Salad Suppers

ALSO BY ANDREA CHESMAN

Simply Healthful Skillet Suppers

Simply Healthful Pasta Salads

Sun-Dried Tomatoes!

Salsas!

Summer in a Jar: Making Pickles, Jams, and More

Pickles and Relishes: 150 Recipes from Apples to Zucchini

Salad Suppers

Fresh Inspirations for Satisfying One-Dish Meals

Andrea Chesman

ILLUSTRATIONS BY KATHLEEN KINKOPF

CHAPTERS™

CHAPTERS PUBLISHING LTD., SHELBURNE, VT 05482

Published by Chapters Publishing, Ltd., 2085 Shelburne Road, Shelburne, VT 05482

Library of Congress Cataloging-in-Publication Data
Chesman, Andrea.
    Salad suppers: fresh inspirations for satisfying one-dish meals /
by Andrea Chesman; illustrated by Kathleen Kinkopf.
    p.   cm.
    Includes index.
    ISBN 1-57630-028-5 (softcover)
    1. Salads. 2. Entrées (Cookery)   I. Title.
    TX740.C393 1997
    641.8'3—DC21   96-37469

Printed and bound in Canada by
Best Book Manufacturers, Inc.

Designed by Susan McClellan

To Richard

Acknowledgments

MANY PEOPLE HAVE HELPED ME IN MY QUEST for the best produce and the most inspiring recipes. My special thanks go to Richard, Rory and Sam, who tasted day in and day out for more than a year. Marjorie Sussman of Orb Weaver Farm in Monkton, Vermont, took me out into the fields and changed my outlook on lettuce forever. Many of my salads were based on Orb Weaver Farm's delicious organic lettuces and vegetables. Nola Kevra of Nola's Secret Garden in Ripton, Vermont, visited with me at her not-so-secret greenhouse and provided me with much inspiration. The folks at Middlebury Natural Foods Co-op were particularly accommodating about special orders. I thank them all.

In the making of this book, Rux Martin has been editor extraordinaire, and Doe Coover has been agent extraordinaire. Both have my deepest appreciation.

Contents

Introduction

WHAT'S FOR SUPPER, MOM?" my son yells, as he bangs through the kitchen door at the end of a summer's day. "I don't know," I say. "Let's see what the garden has to offer."

This is one of our favorite rituals: the collection of the harvest. We head out, each of us lugging a big woven basket, and pick whatever is ready—one day asparagus, one day peas. Then carrots and beans and zucchini. And later still, tomatoes, peppers, eggplant, corn. My son is an enthusiastic harvester, though his basket doesn't show it. He eats just about as fast as he picks.

What I pick, however, forms the basis of our favorite sort of meal: salad suppers. At our house, these are hearty, one-dish meals that include lots of fresh vegetables and are usually served cold or at room temperature. They can start with a bed of dressed greens, cooked grains or even beans. Vegetables, usually raw but sometimes roasted, grilled or lightly steamed, provide the flavors, colors and texture. Sometimes the focus of the dish is meat, fish or chicken. However they are constructed, salad suppers are meant to satisfy hungry appetites while providing nourishing, healthful food. They are also meant to please the eye, since a meal based on fresh vegetables is inevitably lovely. And they minimize the time spent in preparation: Salad suppers are easy, quick to make and ideal for when the weather is hot.

Salads also make great centerpieces for entertaining. Often the different ingredients can be prepared in advance, and the salad assembled and dressed at the last minute. Grain-based salads, in particular, are wonderful to bring to picnics and potlucks; they transport well and can be stretched to feed a crowd. Whatever the salad, it can be served up in huge quantities in big bowls or arranged on individual plates for a more elegant presentation. Garnishing the plate is rarely necessary to add visual appeal, though the last-minute addition of an edible nasturtium blossom or a sprig of fresh herbs is a pretty touch.

If I were to confine my salad days to the warm weather when my northern New England garden is producing, I would be limited indeed. I enjoy these suppers year-round, while still managing to rely on locally grown foods as much as possible. In the summer, I have an endless array of fresh vegetables from which to choose. With the first frost, I say good-bye to good-tasting local tomatoes, but fresh local greens are available from March through November even here in the northern regions, thanks to greenhouse technologies. Elsewhere, the season for fresh greens is longer. And if they don't look so great, a salad supper can be based on rice, beans or pasta and still satisfy the urge for fresh-tasting foods in the winter months. One of my favorite cold-weather salads, for example, is made with wild rice and wild mushrooms. Another winter standby is a noodle salad made with Korean kimchee (pickled cabbage) and tofu.

WHETHER IT'S AN ASIAN NOODLE SALAD or a Mediter-ranean rice salad, some of my favorites are ethnic in ori-gin. I often start with a classic, such as Spanish paella. To transform a traditional dish like this into a salad, I punch up the characteristic flavors and simplify the cooking. Because they are served at room temperature, salads require bold flavors, relying on sprightly fresh herbs or the heat of a chili pepper. Other salads make use of the signature ingredients of various cuisines. For a Mediterranean touch, I may toss in basil, arugula, garlic and capers. For a hint of Southeast Asia, I dress the salad with an oil-free combination of fish sauce, vinegar, sugar and cilantro.

Since salads are generally based on fresh or quickly cooked ingredients, flavors don't get lost or muted in the mix. If you've never had a chance to taste chipotle chilies (smoke-dried jalapeños)—a common ingredient in many Mexican dishes—try them in the Smoky Black Bean Salad (page 44) to get a feel for how to add smoke and gentle heat to food. Cooking rice in coconut milk, as I do in Jamaican-Style Rice and Pea Salad (page 57), gives a tropical or Southeast Asian spirit.

Whatever the composition of your salad or its country of origin, you don't want the dressing to overwhelm everything. Use a light hand. I prefer to start with a high-quality, high-flavor oil, such as extra-virgin olive oil, and extend it with chicken broth or white wine, adding moisture but not fat. A light, slightly sweet vinegar, such as rice wine or balsamic, requires less oil to balance its acidity than a sharper one, such as cider vinegar. Creamy dressings can be made with nonfat buttermilk or yogurt. I've even developed a few dressings based on such ingredients as salsa and mango chutney.

The salads in this collection represent a broad range of vegetables, grains and meats. (Pasta salads are a particular love of mine, and many of my favorite recipes are compiled in another volume, *Simply Healthful Pasta Salads*.) There are pasta salads here, too—and much more. What I've happily discovered is that whether the dish is a feast of vegetables, as in Roasted Vegetable Salad (page 34), or a celebration of spring, such as Warm Asparagus and New Potato Salad with Pan-Seared Trout (page 94), or a crafty combination of leftovers, like Turkey and Greens with Cranberry Vinaigrette (page 122), salad suppers jazz up the most weary palates and provide a carnival of flavors and textures that everyone—including the most finicky child—can enjoy.

Chapter One

Salad Fixings

THE BEST SALADS begin with outstanding fresh vegetables. A few years ago, it seemed you had to live on the West Coast, or at least in New York or another big city, to have access to great food. Now, even the smallest of supermarkets boasts acceptable produce, and spectacular stuff can be found in farmer's markets and food co-ops.

Experienced cooks insist that selecting the right ingredients is the foundation of their skill. The simpler the food, the more important its quality. This is especially true of salads, which don't get the benefit of cooking to enhance taste. It is even more true of low-fat salads, in which lighter dressings must carry the flavor. One might have been able to get away with iceberg lettuce and out-of-season tomatoes when they were buried under a thick blanket of blue cheese dressing and served alongside steak and fries. But when the dressing is a whisper of olive oil, an anointment of vinegar and a sprinkling of herbs, you need to start with the richest oil, the finest vinegar and an uncompromising assortment of spunky greens.

I'm a great believer in taste tests to help me with product selection, but I've found you really can't rely on anyone else's judgments. For products like oils and vinegars, I enjoy reading the results of tastings conducted by various magazines and newspapers. The ones done by *Cook's Illustrated* (Boston Common Press, 17 Station Street, Box 569, Brookline, MA 02147) have been particularly useful and often have suggested new brands to try. When *Cook's* panel taste-tested red wine vinegars (in the September/October 1993 issue), for example, they came up with a surprising first choice: a national brand for under $2 a bottle that outranked even a $20 Italian import. I was glad to have the tip, but in the end, it is only my opinion that counts in my kitchen—judges are rarely unanimous anyway. I like to buy recommended brands and then make my own decisions—in this way, I have a favorite extra-virgin olive oil, a preferred mustard, a red wine vinegar and so on.

A Guide to Greens—and Reds

BASED ON TESTS—including one of lettuces conducted right in the field—I have my own favorite mix of salad greens. Supermarket lettuces are so far from fresh that they've pretty much lost whatever flavor nuances they once had, so a choice of greens from those produce shelves often has more to do with texture and color considerations than with taste. At the farmer's market, I can select Lolla Rossa, a frilly red loose leaf. I always include arugula in my mix when I can get it; I love its zip. I like radicchio for its color. A bitter green, such as curly endive, provides a final note of flavor.

Many of the recipes in this book call for "mixed salad greens." That's because the best combination will be the greens that you like to eat, or the ones that are fresh and vibrant in the market. It makes little sense to prescribe exact lettuces and greens for each salad. Salad making is not, after all, rocket science.

When you are feeling flush, you may want to go to your favorite produce stand and buy an assortment of greens. Sample them plain or with a light dressing of extra-virgin olive oil, red wine vinegar, and salt and pepper. With the knowledge you gain from your taste tests, you should be able to construct your own ideal salad mix. When putting together a blend of greens, look for a balance of taste and textures and a variety of colors. A generous base of lettuce will provide a mild, sweet, crunchy background against which you can play the peppery greens (arugula, dandelion greens and watercress), the cabbagy greens (cabbages, bok choy, mustard greens, mizuna) and the bitter chicories (Belgium endive, curly endive, radicchio).

Here are some of the greens you are most likely to encounter:

Arugula. With a distinctively peppery and slightly bitter flavor, arugula stands out in a salad mix. People either love it or hate it. It has small, lobed, dark green leaves on stems that should be discarded if tough. Arugula is quite perishable and will keep in the refrigerator for two to three days. It is not available year-round (watercress can be substituted as needed), but it is worth stocking when it is, for a handful in any salad adds character. It is easily grown from seed, if you can provide cool enough temperatures and water. Arugula grown under stress—or mishandled at the market—will be very sharp-tasting. Arugula is the Italian name for this green; look for it also under the names "rocket" and "roquette."

Belgian endive. These slightly bitter-tasting greens are grown in the dark so they never develop much color. The white spear-shaped leaves with yellow tips come in tightly packed heads and are especially desirable in composed salads, where you can take advantage of their shape by stuffing them or arranging them petal-fashion around a plate. Look for firm specimens; limp Belgian endive is probably old and will be quite bitter. Witloof chicory is another name by which this green is known.

Bok choy. In the Chinese cabbage family, bok choy has long, white stems fringed with green leaves. Bok choy adds a crisp, refreshing note to a salad. Look for firm, unblemished specimens, and avoid limp bok choy, which will be bland-tasting or bitter.

Cabbage. When buying a mix of greens, don't forget to include cabbage on occasion for its crisp texture and slightly sharp flavor. Red varieties offer the bonus of beautiful color; Chinese napa cabbage adds sweetness.

Curly endive. These days you may see this frizzy-leafed green called by its French name, "frisée," or it may be known as "chicory." By any name, it has a loose head with dark frilly leaves on the outside and paler ones toward the center. The flavor is quite bitter; select pale-colored heads, which are milder.

Dandelion greens. The dandelion greens found in the produce section are usually not as strong-tasting as the ones in your lawn. These greens add a slightly bitter, spicy flavor and are a particularly good choice for a wilted salad with a warm dressing.

Escarole. In the chicory family, escarole has broader leaves than curly endive but tastes similar. Like curly endive, the leaves on the outer edge of the rosette are darker and more strongly flavored.

Lettuce. There are dozens of different lettuce varieties sold by specialty growers, but they fall into four general types. Crisp-head lettuces, such as iceberg, form a firm, round head that can be held for up to a week in the refrigerator. Each head contains about 90 percent water by weight, which accounts for its insipid taste. Alone, these lettuces make a bland salad, but in a mix of greens, they add a crisp texture and sweet flavor. Also, the leaves form the perfect base for a taco salad.

Cos, or romaine-type, lettuces have long, narrow leaves that are dark on the outside and lighter and crisper at the interior of the head. They offer more flavor than iceberg lettuces, while still being crisp and sweet. Romaine is the lettuce of choice for Caesar salads. Look for red romaine at specialty farmstands for extra color.

Butterhead lettuces include Boston lettuce, butter lettuce, Bibb lettuce and Kentucky limestone lettuce. Their leaves are distinctively soft and crumpled, with a mild, sweet flavor and a buttery texture. Butterhead lettuces are quite delicate and wilt almost as soon as they are dressed. Nonetheless, I like to include some in my basic salad mix because they add a certain luxuriousness— and matched with avocado, they taste sinfully rich. A red Boston lettuce, known as Carmona, is unusually sweet and flavorful.

Loose-leaf lettuces offer the most variety in terms of leaf shape and color. At the supermarket, you may find just "red leaf lettuce" and "green leaf lettuce." At a farmstand, you may be regaled with Salad Bowl, Ruby, Oakleaf, Lolla Rossa and Lolla Bianco. In general, these lettuces are mild, sweet and somewhat crisp, with colors ranging from pale green to deeply red. However, it is well worth tasting the different varieties to see which you prefer, when you have the choice. Oakleaf, with its distinctively lobed leaves, for example, is lovely to look at, but not very flavorful. On the hand, Lolla Rossa and Lolla Bianco are two exceptionally tasty varieties. They also have particularly frilly leaves, which add much texture to a salad.

Mâche. This green is also known as corn salad or field lettuce (because it is found wild in cornfields) and lamb's lettuce (because the small, tender, velvety leaves are said to resemble a lamb's tongue). The flavor is delicate and rather nutty, and this green goes well with walnut or hazelnut oils. Mâche is usually expensive because it is extremely perishable.

Mesclun. From a French word meaning "mixture," mesclun (or sometimes "mesclum") is a combination of baby greens and herbs. You pay a premium price because the harvesting involves extra work and because the farmer picks the leaves when they are very small, thus reducing the yield per acre—but the extra cost is usually worth it. The mix may include butter lettuce, mâche, arugula, red leaf lettuce, baby mustard leaves, spinach and edible herbs, such as chervil. A very easy-to-make, special-occasion salad supper can be made with a bed of lightly dressed mesclun on top of which you can place grilled meat, fish or fowl.

Mizuna. As more Asian ingredients have made their way into our kitchens, mizuna (pronounced mee-ZOO-na) has been adopted as a salad vegetable. It has glossy dark green feathery leaves with juicy white stems and a fairly mild flavor. Mizuna is also used in stir-fries.

Pea Shoots. Once found only in Chinese markets, pea shoots have become more common on the produce shelves of many food stores, and they are worth buying when they appear. These are the tender leaves of garden peas that have been prevented from flowering or fruiting to encourage the growth of their small, round leaves. They are mild in flavor. Pea shoots stay fresh for only a few days and should be kept in plastic bags in the refrigerator.

Radicchio. Perhaps the most beautiful "green" in the salad bowl, radicchio has brilliant, ruby-colored leaves with white veins in a small, tight head. The leaves can be used as bowls for dips. Radicchio adds a slightly bitter, cabbagelike flavor and lots of color.

Spinach. Tender, young spinach with dark green, glossy leaves and a somewhat astringent flavor are a familiar sight in the salad bowl, alone or mixed with other greens. The crinkly leaves of certain varieties hold dirt, so wash thoroughly. Discard large stems, which tend to be stringy and tough. Spinach salads can stand up to assertive dressings—anything from soy-based vinaigrettes to creamy blue cheese. They also do well in warm, wilted salads.

Sprouts. The sprouted seeds of alfalfa, mung beans, radishes and sunflowers aren't really greens, but they are often treated as such in a salad. Sprouts add considerable interest for their texture and appearance. Alfalfa sprouts are mild in flavor, mung bean sprouts are juicy and almost sweet, while radish sprouts can be quite peppery. When buying sprouts, make sure they are crisp, with no signs of yellowing or browning, indicating age.

Watercress. A spicy-flavored green with dark-green lobed leaves, it adds character to any salad. Although it has its own peppery flavor, you can substitute it for the more difficult-to-find arugula.

Buying Greens

I T WOULD BE CONVENIENT for the unwary consumer if greens could go from prime condition to visibly inedible without undergoing a gradual deterioration in taste, texture and nutrient value. But that is not the case. It would be nice, too, if supermarket-produce managers would either acquire the knack of ordering only what can be quickly sold, or else accept the necessity of discarding vegetables past their prime. Since old greens will be either bitter and limp or bland and watery, let the buyer beware.

Greens should look and smell fresh and be vibrant in color, with no wilted, dry or yellowing leaves. The stems should be crisp, not limp or tough. If they have been cut away from the roots, examine the cut ends. If they are brown, slimy or very dry, the greens were likely harvested a long time ago. Pick up the bunch; if it feels excessively light, don't buy it. The heavier it is, the fresher. Try to purchase only what you can use within a few days.

Depending on whether greens are to be the main feature of your salad or used as a base for other ingredients, you will need anywhere from 2 to 4 cups per person. Figure that 1 pound yields about 6 cups. When measuring greens by the cup, do not pack them in.

Storing and Restoring Greens

To wash or not to wash: It really depends on just which greens you are about to put into storage.

The worst thing you can do to store-bought greens is just stick them in the refrigerator, twist ties and all, after you buy them. Remove the twist ties, pull off any yellowed or bruised leaves, pat the fresh leaves dry, and tuck away into a plastic bag in the vegetable-crisper drawer. It is especially important to make sure the leaves are reasonably dry when they go into the refrigerator. Sometimes they can be quite drenched from the sprays that are applied to keep them fresh-looking in the supermarket. Wet leaves will rot.

Greens that are already limp will keep longer if they are washed in cool water and dried before they are refrigerated. I find that my own homegrown lettuce keeps much longer if washed immediately after harvesting. Specialty greens bought at a farmstand are likely to have been cleaned already. Washed and bagged loose greens, such as mesclun, should not be rinsed before storage—that step has already been performed, which is part of the reason you are paying a premium price. Should you wash again before serving? The choice is yours. If you suspect the greens are harboring dirt, by all means do so.

Because they grow low to the ground and have plenty of little folds in the leaves, greens are excellent dirt catchers. And there's nothing appealing about a gritty salad, so it is important to wash greens thoroughly and carefully. The best way to do this is to fill a sink or large bowl with cool water. Add the greens and swish them around with your hands. Let the greens stand in the water for a few minutes to allow the dirt to settle. Then lift them out to dry. If they are exceptionally dirty, you may want to re-peat this process.

The best way to dry greens is with a salad spinner. Normally I don't endorse owning a space-taking, single-use tool—but I make an exception for a three-piece salad spinner, which costs be-tween $15 and $20. Spinners have a round perforated baskets that are set in an outer basket. The basket with the holes is loosely filled with greens, covered, and the gears in the lid are cranked to spin the basket rapidly. The centrifugal force pulls the greens to the basket's sides while the water is flung out through the slots. Spinners come in a few different styles—with a hand crank or a pull cord. The pull-cord models work more efficiently, but the cords tend to break with heavy use. You can greatly extend the life of your cord by making sure it is completely dry before putting it away. Some models have drainage holes on the bottom and an opening in the top to allow you to wash under running water, spin dry and drain in one container. The washing action only works with small loads of greens that are not excessively dirty. You can also dry greens by shaking off excess moisture and blotting them dry with a clean dish towel.

Store the clean, dry greens wrapped loosely in dry paper tow-els or cotton towels in plastic bags. Keep the bags in the crisper drawer of the refrigerator. Or, if your refrigerator boasts empty shelves, store the greens right in the salad spinner. Herbs and greens that still have their roots attached (often watercress, arugula, cilantro and basil are sold this way) can be placed in a glass of wa-ter like a bouquet. Most herbs can then be placed in the refriger-ator, but basil and cilantro will last longer at room temperature.

Because greens are 90 percent water, they are prone to wilting. To restore homegrown greens picked in the heat of day, try this trick: Place the stems in a jar of water to which you have added a tablespoon of lemon juice. Refrigerate for one hour. If you aren't going to use the greens immediately, wrap in paper towels and store in plastic bags as above.

Other Salad Vegetables

CHOOSE TOMATOES THAT ARE FIRM, well-shaped and fragrant. Store them at room temperature—never in the refrigerator—and use within a few days. Left at room temperature, a tomato will continue to ripen. At temperatures below 50°F, however, it will turn red, but it will never become juicy and sweet. Even a completely ripe tomato will taste better at room temperature and will keep for one or two days. If you are worried about your tomatoes rotting, test the temperature of the butter compartment in your refrigerator. Often it will be between 50° and 60°F, and it will hold two to four tomatoes at a time.

For a change of pace, try arranging a taste test, perhaps with a group of gardeners. Heirloom tomatoes may lack the characteristics that large-scale market farmers require—disease resistance and high yields—but they are often unbelievably flavorful. Once you've tasted some of these varieties, you may look at your own garden with renewed interest. Or talk to your favorite farmer: Many growers would be interested in planting different varieties if they were guaranteed a market for them.

After the local harvest, consider omitting tomatoes from your salads altogether. Or you may want to switch to plum tomatoes and cherry tomatoes for a slight gain in flavor over the standard varieties.

Corn is another vegetable that should be eaten in season. Although today's sugar-enhanced varieties have been bred to slow down the natural process that causes the sugar to convert to starch, what you get is a sweet vegetable with very little taste. I suggest sticking with your local farmer and asking for heirloom varieties for salads.

When buying corn, insist on freshly picked. Choose ears that are bright green, with crisp husks. The silks should be dry, not soggy, and not limp. Do not buy prehusked corn: Husking speeds deterioration. Keep corn in the husk in the refrigerator until you are ready to use it. The kernels do not need to be cooked for salad. In a pinch, frozen corn can be used, but add a little sugar to the dressing.

In part because they are available year-round, cucumbers are highly popular in salads. I have a strong preference for English (aka hothouse or European) cucumbers, which are longer than the standard varieties (up to 18 inches long) and thinner and have smaller seeds. They are usually found wrapped in plastic, but not waxed, so the skins remain edible. With the skins left on, the cucumbers have more flavor, texture and color. But if you prefer the inexpensive waxed ones, peel and seed them before slicing.

As for potato salads, Red Bliss and new potatoes hold their shape well and have the best flavor for salads, although you can use any all-purpose variety.

For salads made with dried beans, I generally opt for the convenience of canned. While home-cooked beans inevitably have better texture, the appeal of simply opening a can is overwhelming. Rinse and drain canned beans well before using.

Whatever the vegetable, don't be afraid to substitute one for another. Asparagus can be replaced by green beans once the local harvest is over. Jerusalem artichokes fill in for jicama when you want something sweet and crunchy. Carrots and red bell peppers are often interchangeable. No matter what the recipe, your salad will taste best with fresh, local produce.

Oils

OIL IS THE CARRIER OF THE DRESSING'S FLAVOR. Olive oil is preferred for most salads. As a monounsaturated fat, it is the most healthful one, along with canola and almond oils, because monounsaturates are thought to be effective in lowering blood cholesterol. (Nonetheless, a fat is a fat, and when plenty of moisture in a salad is needed, I usually extend the oil with chicken broth. In vinaigrettes, I often trick out the oil with a combination of broth and white wine.)

Olive oil is graded by the processors to distinguish it by quality and flavor. Extra-virgin olive oil is the finest and fruitiest and also the most expensive; it is the best choice because it imparts the most taste. It goes especially well with strongly flavored greens. Spanish, Greek and southern Italian olive oils tend to be fruitier than those from Tuscany and Provence. Try a few brands and notice whether the flavor is harsh or smooth, bland or fruity. Is the finish a little peppery, and do you like that? If you like the taste of the oil drizzled on bread, you will like it in a dressing.

Nut oils are often good in salads. Walnut and hazelnut oils are strongly flavored, while almond oil is light and sweet. Peanut oil is rather neutral. With the exception of peanut oil, nut oils tend to be quite perishable and will become rancid quickly. If your oil develops an off flavor, discard it. Buy nut oils in the smallest possible quantity and store them in the refrigerator.

Asian sesame oil adds a quintessential "Asian" flavoring to salads. It is made from toasted sesame seeds, as opposed to the lightly colored sesame oil that is found in health food stores, which is made from untoasted seeds and tastes much more neutral. Asian sesame oil is so distinctive that it is usually used sparingly.

Corn oil, safflower oil, sunflower oil and "salad oil" (a low-grade mixture) are all fairly neutral. Although economical, they add little flavor. I usually avoid these.

Infused oils can make wonderful salad dressings because they impart an intense burst of flavor. Most of these oils start with a neutral-tasting olive or other oil, which is heated with ingredients like basil, rosemary, thyme, garlic, capers, olives, mushrooms, chilies or sun-dried tomatoes. Then the oil stands for a few days to allow the flavors to permeate it. The flavorings are discarded and the infused oil is strained into a fresh bottle. You can buy infused oils at specialty food stores. Feel free to substitute infused oils for the extra-virgin olive oil called for in most salads.

Vinegars

IN TRADITIONAL SALAD DRESSINGS, where the ratio of oil to vinegar may be three or even four parts to one, the vinegar plays a necessary role of balancing the richness. In a lighter dressing, where the oil is kept to a minimum and bland moisture extenders are used, vinegars of more character can contribute crucial flavor. For this reason, full-bodied balsamic vinegar or other red wine vinegars are good picks. Balsamic vinegar, a red wine vinegar, gets its characteristic dark color and mellow sweetness from aging in barrels for at least six years—although inexpensive brands may be nothing more than ordinary red wine vinegar tarted up with caramel food coloring, sugar and vanilla flavoring. Sherry vinegar has a mild, almost sweet flavor. For dressings with an Asian influence, mellow rice wine vinegar adds the right note of gentle acidity.

Herbal vinegars, made by steeping fresh herbs in a wine vinegar, and fruit vinegars—soft fruits added to vinegar—can be substituted for unflavored ones in many recipes. Keep in mind that you want to harmonize tastes, not create cacophony. Flavored vinegars are easily made at home; see page 153.

Final Flourishes

IT'S HARD TO IMAGINE a salad that isn't attractive; a colorful mix of vegetables is always appealing. While most green salads are simply tossed together, many salad suppers are best served "composed"—meaning arranged—whether on individual plates or a serving platter. The base is usually a bed of greens. The greens are lightly dressed only if they are to be topped with dry meats, grains or vegetables; often the dressing, sauce or natural juices of the other ingredients is sufficient to moisten them.

On top of the greens, you will set grains or beans or a piece of meat or fish. The grains can be molded and shaped if a formal look appeals to you. The meat should be sliced thinly and fanned out, giving a more generous appearance as well as allowing more of the natural juices to mingle with the greens. Around the meat or grains, arrange the additional vegetables: tomato wedges or sliced cucumbers, carrots, peppers or green beans.

Taking some extra care to slice vegetables in uniform pieces always enhances a salad's appearance. A mandoline—a stainless-steel cutting tool—does a superior job of slicing, julienning and waffle-cutting. Although you can live your whole life without one, if you love really useful gadgets, or if you have generous friends and family who are willing to indulge you, put the mandoline on your wish list. Don't bother, however, with the less expensive plastic or wooden models, which will buckle, warp and fight with you.

Salads rarely require a fussy garnish. A sprinkling of chopped scallions or fresh herbs is enough. A sprig of the herb used in the dressing is also a nice touch. On occasion, an edible flower blossom can be eye-catching—and reinforces the idea that the salad came right out of the garden. Nasturtium leaves and flowers are my favorite because they taste as good (peppery) as they look (colorful, with distinctively round leaves). Violets have a delicate flavor that works well with most salads, and the purple blossoms look smashing against greens. Rose petals and calendula flowers (pot marigold) can also supply grace notes.

While all of the salads in this book are meant to serve as a complete meal, sometimes a little more is desired. Bread is always a natural accompaniment, providing a welcome contrast in texture and taste as well as acting as a great sponge for sopping up that last drop of delicious dressing. Flatbreads, too, make excellent accompaniments, and many salads can serve as fillings for pitas, tortillas and chapatis. When appetites are extra-large or the occasion extra-special, a light soup makes a nice opening to the meal. Likewise, a smooth and creamy dessert is often just the right conclusion.

Chapter Two

Simply Vegetables

Tomato Salad with Corn, Roasted Peppers and Fresh Mozzarella

Makes 4 to 6 servings

THIS FRESH FEAST of grilled corn, vine-ripened tomatoes and fragrant basil is the perfect way to end a hot summer day—don't even think of making this recipe until the local harvest is ready. Sharp-tasting arugula provides a peppery contrast to the sweetness of the vegetables.

8	ears fresh corn
3	pounds (about 6 medium) vine-ripened tomatoes, chopped
1	Vidalia or similar sweet onion, thinly sliced
2	large garlic cloves, minced
½	cup chopped fresh basil
2	tablespoons extra-virgin olive oil
2	tablespoons balsamic vinegar
	Salt and pepper
2	yellow bell peppers
8-12	slices French or whole wheat bread
4	cups chopped arugula
½	pound fresh mozzarella cheese, thinly sliced

1. At least 1 hour before serving, soak the corn (still in the husks) in water to cover. Combine the tomatoes, onion, garlic, basil, oil and vinegar in a large salad bowl. Season with salt and pepper to taste. Set aside. Prepare a medium-hot fire in a charcoal or gas grill, with the rack set 3 to 4 inches above the coals.

2. When the coals are medium-hot, drain the corn and grill until done, 15 to 20 minutes; it will be tender and slightly charred. Shuck the corn and remove the kernels from the cob, using a sharp knife. Add to the salad bowl.

3. Roast the bell peppers over the hot coals, turning, until charred. Place in a paper bag to steam for 15 minutes. Peel, remove seeds, chop and add to the salad bowl.

4. Toast the bread over the coals until golden, turning once. Cut into cubes.

5. Just before serving, add the arugula and bread cubes to the salad and toss to mix. Spoon the salad onto individual salad plates or a large serving plate. Top with the mozzarella cheese and serve immediately.

Roasted Vegetable Salad

**Makes
4 servings**

A FEAST OF vegetables! The caramelized mixture sits on top of a lightly dressed green salad with a crumbling of salty feta cheese. The sweet and salty flavors, as well as the contrasting colors and textures, contribute to an enjoyable meal.

1½	pounds new red potatoes, cut into wedges
1	pound beets, julienned
½	pound baby carrots, left whole
½	pound green beans, chopped
1	small onion, slivered
1	whole garlic bulb, cloves separated and peeled
1	fennel bulb, julienned
1	red bell pepper, cut into strips
3	tablespoons chopped mixed fresh herbs
3	tablespoons olive oil
¾	cup defatted chicken broth or more as needed
	Salt and pepper to taste
10	cups torn mixed salad greens (include some radicchio for color)
1	large tomato, cut into wedges
2	teaspoons balsamic vinegar
½	cup crumbled feta cheese

1. Preheat the oven to 450°F.

2. In a large bowl, combine the vegetables, herbs, 2 tablespoons of the oil, broth, salt and pepper. Toss well. Arrange in a single layer on two baking sheets or in a very large roasting pan.

3. Roast the vegetables for about 45 minutes, stirring every 15 minutes or so, or until they are well browned. Remove from the oven and let cool to room temperature.

4. Combine the salad greens and tomato in a bowl. Toss with the remaining 1 tablespoon oil and the vinegar. Arrange on a large serving platter. Sprinkle on the feta cheese. Spoon the vegetables on top. Serve at once.

Grilled Vegetable Pasta Salad

Makes 4 to 6 servings

Utter simplicity and clean, uncomplicated flavors are the hallmarks of this outstanding low-fat salad. Vegetables are lightly coated with olive oil, garlic and rosemary, then grilled. They are then tossed with pasta and basil. A little salt, pepper and lemon juice bring out the delicious caramelized taste.

1	pound dried small pasta (farfalle, shells, twists, orecchiette)
3	tablespoons extra-virgin olive oil or herb-flavored oil
2	garlic cloves
½-1	teaspoon crushed rosemary
1	small head radicchio, quartered
1	small onion, peeled and quartered
1	red bell pepper, cored and halved
1	green bell pepper, cored and halved
1	pound asparagus (in season) or other vegetable (such as green beans or sliced zucchini), trimmed
½	cup chopped fresh basil
	Juice of 1 lemon or more to taste
	Salt and pepper

1. Prepare a medium-hot fire in a charcoal or gas grill, with the rack set 3 to 4 inches above the coals.

2. Cook the pasta in a large pot of boiling, salted water until tender but firm to the bite, about 9 minutes. Drain and rinse thoroughly to cool. Place in a large mixing bowl and toss with 2 teaspoons of the oil.

3. Combine the remaining oil, garlic and rosemary in a small bowl. Prepare the vegetables and toss with the oil. When the coals are medium-hot, grill the vegetables on both sides until just cooked, but not mushy, 5 to 7 minutes; they should be slightly charred but still crisp. As they cook, remove them to a baking sheet, spreading them out so they cool as quickly as possible.

4. When all the vegetables are cooked, cut them into ½-inch pieces. (If desired, the vegetables and pasta can be held in separate containers at room temperature for several hours.)

5. Just before serving, toss the vegetables with the pasta, basil and lemon juice. Season with salt and pepper to taste. Serve at room temperature.

Pasta Salad
with Summer Vegetables

Makes 4 to 5 servings

GOAT CHEESE makes a rich addition to this salad of pasta, roasted eggplant and zucchini. Marinated tomatoes are combined with basil and mint for a light dressing.

4	medium-to-large tomatoes, diced
½	cup chopped fresh basil
¼	cup chopped fresh mint
2	garlic cloves, minced
¼	cup defatted chicken broth
2	tablespoons balsamic vinegar
3	tablespoons extra-virgin olive oil
	Salt and pepper
1¼	pounds eggplant, peeled and diced
1¼	pounds small zucchini, diced
1	pound dried shells or farfalle
4	ounces soft fresh goat cheese

1. Preheat the oven to 450°F.

2. In a medium bowl, combine the tomatoes, basil, mint, garlic, broth, vinegar, 2 tablespoons of the oil and salt and pepper to taste. Set aside.

3. Spray a shallow roasting pan with olive-oil nonstick cooking spray. Add the eggplant and zucchini and mist with more nonstick spray. Roast for 15 to 20 minutes, turning occasionally, or until the vegetables are soft and browned, but not mushy.

4. Meanwhile, cook the pasta in a large pot of boiling, salted water until tender but firm to the bite, 9 to 12 minutes. Drain and rinse thoroughly to cool. Place in a large mixing bowl and toss with the remaining 1 tablespoon of the oil.

5. Add the vegetables to the tomato mixture and let cool to room temperature.

6. Just before serving, add the vegetables to the pasta and toss. Crumble the goat cheese and add to the salad, toss again and serve.

Mediterranean Salad Plate

**Makes
4 servings**

FOR THIS SALAD plate, mounds of Middle Eastern baba ghanoush (a boldly flavored combination of eggplant, tahini and garlic) and Greek tzaziki (a light relish of chopped cucumber in a yogurt dill sauce) are placed over greens. The platter is garnished with pita bread, olives, cherry tomatoes, feta cheese, peperonata, pickled vegetables or even stuffed grape leaves.

Baba Ghanoush

2 pounds eggplant
1 red bell pepper
4 garlic cloves
   Juice of 1 lemon
¼ cup tahini (sesame paste)
   Salt and pepper to taste

Tzaziki

1 English cucumber, halved lengthwise and thinly sliced
¼ cup finely chopped red onion
2 garlic cloves, minced
2 tablespoons chopped fresh dill
1 cup plain nonfat yogurt
   Salt and pepper to taste

Green Salad

8 cups torn mixed salad greens
1 carrot, shredded or cut into curls
2 tablespoons olive oil
1 tablespoon red wine vinegar
   Salt and pepper to taste

4 round pita pockets
   Cherry tomatoes, feta cheese cubes, olives or olive salad, pickled vegetables or peperonata (optional)

1. To make the baba ghanoush: Preheat the broiler or prepare a medium-hot fire in a charcoal or gas grill. With a fork, prick the eggplant in several places. Broil or grill, turning occasionally, until evenly charred, about 20 minutes. At the same time, broil or grill the red pepper for about 5 minutes, turning occasionally, until evenly charred. Place the charred pepper in a paper bag and seal the bag. Set aside for about 10 minutes. Peel, remove seeds, slice into strips and set aside.

2. Puree the garlic in a food processor fitted with a steel blade. When the eggplant has cooled, halve it and scoop out the flesh, add to the food processor and puree. Add lemon, tahini, salt and pepper and process until smooth. Transfer to a small bowl and set aside. (The baba ghanoush can be made up to 1 day in advance. Bring to room temperature before serving.)

3. To make the tzaziki: Combine all the ingredients in a small bowl. Set aside.

4. To make the green salad: Combine the greens and carrot in a mixing bowl. Drizzle the oil, vinegar, salt and pepper over the salad. Toss well.

5. To assemble the salad: Preheat the oven to 300°F. Wrap the pita pockets in aluminum foil and heat for about 10 minutes.

6. Spread the green salad on a large platter. Mound the baba ghanoush on the greens. Arrange the roasted pepper strips on top. Mound the tzaziki on the greens. If you like, garnish the plate with tomatoes, cheese, olives and/or pickled vegetables. Pass the warmed pita pockets at the table.

THE INDIVIDUAL components of this dish can be prepared ahead, making it a great centerpiece for a party table—or a convenient supper on a hot night.

Hummus Salad Plate

**Makes
4 servings**

Hummus is a Middle Eastern dip made with pureed chickpeas seasoned with lemon juice, garlic and tahini (sesame paste) or sesame oil. It makes a great dip for vegetables or can be stuffed into a pita pocket, along with lettuce and tomatoes, for a hearty vegetarian sandwich. Here it is presented on a bed of greens and sliced tomatoes, garnished with chopped scallions and red pepper rings, with pita pockets to accompany it.

Hummus

1	cup chopped fresh parsley
4	garlic cloves
2	15-ounce cans chickpeas, rinsed and drained
½	cup tahini
4-6	tablespoons fresh lemon juice
1-4	tablespoons water (optional)
	Salt and pepper to taste
4	pita pockets, cut into wedges
8	cups torn mixed salad greens
½	English cucumber, sliced, or 1 regular cucumber, peeled and sliced
4	tomatoes, sliced
1	red bell pepper, sliced
¼	cup chopped scallions

1. To make the hummus: Combine the parsley and garlic in a food processor fitted with a steel blade. Process until finely chopped. Add the chickpeas, tahini and lemon juice and process until smooth, adding water as needed, 1 tablespoon at a time, to make a smooth paste. You may have to do this in two batches, depending on the size of your food processor. Taste and adjust the seasonings, adding salt, pepper, garlic and/or additional lemon juice. (The hummus can be refrigerated in a tightly closed container for up to 3 days.)

2. Preheat the oven to 300°F. Wrap the pita pockets in aluminum foil and heat for 10 minutes, or until warmed.

3. Arrange a bed of greens on a platter or individual plates. Mound the hummus in the center. Garnish with the tomatoes, red pepper and chopped scallions. Serve the pita pockets on the side of the plate or pass at the table in a separate basket.

Smoky Black Bean Salad

**Makes
4 servings**

Chipotles en Adobo (pronounced chih-POHT-lays en ah-DOH-boh) is the magical ingredient in these beans and in many other Mexican dishes. The magic comes from the smoke flavor—chipotles are smoke-dried jalapeños. You can find them in dried form or conveniently rehydrated and pureed in a tomato-vinegar sauce, which is what adobo is. I admit to being addicted to chipotles, trying them out in everything from salad dressings (they work!) to corn bread (I don't think so).

1	19-ounce can black beans, rinsed and drained
2	cups diced tomatoes (fresh or canned)
½	green or red bell pepper, chopped
3-4	scallions, chopped
1	tablespoon chipotles en adobo or more to taste
2	tablespoons chopped fresh cilantro
	Salt and pepper to taste
8	cups chopped iceberg lettuce
4	tomatoes, cut into wedges
½	English cucumber, sliced
¼	cup chopped sweet or red onion
1	tablespoon olive oil
1	tablespoon balsamic vinegar
½	cup shredded reduced-fat Cheddar or Monterey Jack cheese
2	cups baked tortilla chips
¼	cup fat-free sour cream
4	black olives, pitted

1. Combine the beans, tomatoes, bell pepper, scallions, chipotles en adobo and cilantro in a medium saucepan and heat over medium-high heat. Taste and adjust the seasonings, adding salt and pepper. Keep warm.

2. In a large bowl, combine the lettuce, tomatoes, cucumber and onion. Season with salt and pepper. Drizzle the oil and vinegar over the vegetables. Toss well.

3. Divide the lettuce mixture among individual plates. Top with the cheese, then with the warm bean mixture. Garnish each plate with tortilla chips. Top each serving with a dollop of sour cream and some sliced olives.

THIS SALAD COMBINES the light crunchy goodness of fresh vegetables with the heartiness of cooked beans. However, the beans are so good and so quick to prepare that you may find yourself serving them without the salad, as a filling for tortillas or a topping for rice.

LOOK FOR CHIPOTLES EN ADOBO in specialty stores where Mexican foods are carried. A good mail-order source is:
Nancy's Specialty Market
P.O. Box 530
Newmarket, NH 03857
(800) 462-6291.

Kimchee Noodle Salad with Tofu

Makes 4 to 6 servings

KIMCHEE is a Korean pickle—hot and sour. It is usually made with cabbage, turnips and carrots or some variation of the three. Kimchee is eaten daily in most Korean homes, and many Westerners find it addictive. I know I do—and my husband keeps a bottle in the refrigerator at work. It adds pep to all manner of foods. There are those who claim that kimchee is the solution to all problems related to digestion. I don't know about that, but this salad is rich in good-for-you fiber and vitamins.

1	pound firm tofu
2	tablespoons toasted sesame seeds (optional)
2	tablespoons sesame oil
2	tablespoons soy sauce or to taste
2	tablespoons mirin (sweet Japanese rice wine)
1	pound dried vermicelli
¼	pound (1 cup) snow peas, trimmed
2	scallions, chopped
2	cups cabbage kimchee
	Salt to taste

1. Press the tofu to remove excess liquid: Wrap it in a clean dish towel or paper towels. Place it on a plate and weight it with a cast-iron skillet or a heavy plate with a weight on top, such as a filled juice can. Let stand for 30 minutes; drain.

2. Meanwhile, if you are using the sesame seeds, toast them: Place them in a small, dry skillet over medium heat for about 5 minutes, stirring often. Remove from the heat as soon as they begin to turn golden. Do not allow them to scorch; burned seeds taste bitter. Set aside.

3. Dice the pressed tofu. In a large salad bowl, combine 1 tablespoon of the sesame oil, 2 tablespoons soy sauce and mirin. Add the tofu and toss to coat with the marinade. Marinate for about 30 minutes.

4. Cook the vermicelli in a large pot of boiling, salted water according to the package directions, 4 to 6 minutes, until tender but firm to the bite. Rinse under running water to cool. Toss with the remaining 1 tablespoon sesame oil.

5. Add the noodles, snow peas and scallions to the tofu. Toss well. Add the kimchee and toss again. Taste and add soy sauce or salt, if needed. Serve garnished with toasted sesame seeds, if desired.

LOOK FOR KIMCHEE in health food stores and where Asian ingredients are sold. If you have a choice, the kimchee that is kept in the refrigerated cases is usually fresher and crisper than that found in the canned-goods section.

Gado Gado

**Makes
4 servings**

THIS INDONESIAN classic of lightly steamed and raw vegetables served with a spicy peanut sauce is a vegetarian's delight. The flavors of Southeast Asia—peanuts, coconut milk, ginger and chilies—combine in the dipping sauce (which is called Gado Gado). The garnish of sautéed tofu cubes adds just enough substance so no one leaves the table feeling unsatisfied. Serve with French bread to mop up any extra sauce.

Peanut Sauce

½	cup soy sauce
¼	cup rice wine vinegar
2	tablespoons sugar
1	tablespoon grated gingerroot
4	tablespoons reduced-fat peanut butter
½	cup "light" coconut milk
1	tablespoon chili paste with garlic
1	pound firm tofu

Vegetables

¾	pound new potatoes, cut into wedges
2	broccoli spears, sliced lengthwise
2	carrots, cut into sticks
¼	pound green beans, trimmed
¼	pound (1 cup) snow peas, trimmed
1	tablespoon sesame oil
2	shallots, diced
1	tablespoon soy sauce
4	cups torn spinach, tough stems removed, or torn mixed greens
½	pint cherry tomatoes

1. To make the peanut sauce: Combine all the ingredients in a blender and process until smooth. Transfer to a small serving bowl and set aside.

2. Press the tofu to remove excess liquid: Wrap it in a clean dish towel or paper towels. Place it on a plate and weight it with a cast-iron skillet or a heavy plate with a weight on top, such as a filled juice can. Let stand for 30 minutes; drain.

3. Meanwhile, prepare the vegetables: Boil the potatoes in water to cover until just tender, about 5 minutes. Drain and set aside. Lightly blanch or steam the broccoli, carrots, green beans and snow peas until just barely tender. If you have a large enough steamer, steam them together: Once the water is boiling, place the broccoli in the steamer basket. Cover, steam for 1 minute, then add the carrots. Cover and steam for 1 minute more, then add the green beans and snow peas. Cover and steam for 1 minute. Remove from the heat and immediately plunge into ice water to stop the cooking.

4. Cut the pressed tofu into ½-inch cubes. Heat the sesame oil in a large nonstick skillet. Add tofu, shallots and soy sauce and sauté for about 5 minutes, until the tofu is slightly crusty.

5. Arrange the spinach or greens on a large serving plate. Top with a decorative arrangement of potatoes, steamed vegetables and cherry tomatoes. Garnish with the tofu and shallots. Serve the peanut sauce on the side.

YOU CAN MAKE THE sauce with whatever peanut butter you happen to stock—"natural" or whipped, chunky or smooth, reduced-fat or not. Unsweetened coconut milk can be found wherever Asian or Caribbean foods are sold. I prefer Thai Kitchen's "lite" coconut milk, which is the unsweetened milk after the heavier solids are skimmed off.

Russian Beet and Potato Salad

**Makes
4 servings**

Neon, garish, lurid—it's hard to find an exact description for this dazzlingly bright, magenta-colored salad of beets and potatoes in a cream sauce, garnished with chopped hard-cooked eggs. "Delicious" is the best word for it. The sweet beets, which are steamed rather than boiled so they retain their color and flavor, are combined with potatoes, sour cream, dill and horseradish. The cucumber adds an essential crunch. You can easily make a whole meal of this salad with the addition of a dark Russian rye or pumpernickel bread.

3	pounds (about 15) beets, 2½ inches in diameter
1½	pounds potatoes
1	English cucumber, diced
¼	cup chopped fresh dill
¼	cup chopped scallions
1	cup plain nonfat yogurt
1	cup regular or reduced-fat sour cream
2	tablespoons prepared horseradish or to taste
1	tablespoon cider vinegar
	Salt and pepper
2	hard-cooked eggs, chopped

1. Wash the beets. Place in a steaming basket over boiling water, cover and steam, adding more water as needed, for 30 to 40 minutes, or until tender. Plunge the beets into cold water to stop the cooking. Slip off the skins. Cut into ½-inch cubes and place in a large salad bowl.

2. Meanwhile, boil the potatoes in a medium saucepan in water to cover until just tender, 30 to 40 minutes. When cool enough to handle, peel and cut into ½-inch cubes. Add to the salad bowl.

3. Add the cucumber, dill and scallions to the salad bowl. Mix well. Add the yogurt, sour cream, 1 tablespoon horseradish and vinegar. Taste and season with salt, pepper and the remaining 1 tablespoon horseradish as needed. Chill well.

4. Garnish with the chopped eggs and serve.

Tabbouleh

2   cups bulgur
4   cups boiling water
2   cups chopped fresh parsley
1   English cucumber, diced, or 2 regular
    cucumbers, peeled, seeded and diced
2   large tomatoes, seeded and diced
6   scallions, chopped
¼   cup chopped fresh mint or 1 tablespoon dried
3   tablespoons extra-virgin olive oil
    Juice of 1 lemon or more to taste
    Salt and pepper
    Romaine lettuce leaves

Makes 4 to 6 servings

TABBOULEH originated in the Middle East as a parsley salad, with bulgur, or cracked wheat, added for bulk, along with tomatoes and cucumbers. Traditionally, it is dressed with olive oil, lemon and mint. The American interpretation has generally been to make tabbouleh as a grain salad with a generous grace note of parsley. My version is filling enough to serve as a main course.

1. Combine the bulgur and boiling water in a large mixing bowl. Cover and let stand for 15 to 30 minutes, until the grains are tender and most of the water is absorbed. Drain off any excess water.

2. Add the parsley, cucumber, tomatoes, scallions and mint to the bulgur. Toss to mix. Add the oil, lemon juice and season with salt and pepper to taste; toss again. Let stand for 30 to 60 minutes to allow the flavors to blend. Taste and adjust the seasonings, adding more salt, lemon juice or mint as needed.

3. To serve, arrange the romaine in spokes around individual plates or a serving platter and mound the tabbouleh in the center. Diners can use the lettuce leaves to scoop up portions of the tabbouleh.

Couscous "Tabbouleh" with Feta Cheese

Makes 4 to 6 servings

MILD-TASTING couscous gets a bold lift when combined with lemon, mint, feta cheese and parsley. Serve with a basket of assorted warmed flatbreads for a light summer meal. The salad also holds up well for potlucks and will feed a crowd as one of an assortment of dishes.

2 cups instant couscous
1 teaspoon salt
3 cups boiling water
6 scallions, chopped
1 English cucumber, diced
1 15-ounce can chickpeas, rinsed and drained
½ cup crumbled feta cheese
1 cup chopped fresh parsley
¼ cup chopped fresh mint
3 tablespoons extra-virgin olive oil
  Juice of 1-2 lemons
  Salt and pepper to taste
2 large tomatoes, diced

1. Combine the couscous, salt and boiling water in a large mixing bowl. Cover and let stand until the couscous is tender and the water is absorbed, about 10 minutes. Fluff with a fork. Cool to room temperature.

2. Add the scallions, cucumber, chickpeas, feta, parsley and mint and toss gently. (The salad can be held in the refrigerator for several hours at this point.)

3. Before serving, bring the salad to room temperature. Add the oil, 2 tablespoons of the lemon juice, salt and pepper. Add the tomatoes and toss. Taste for seasonings, adding salt, pepper and lemon juice as needed.

Artichoke-Couscous Salad

Makes
4 servings

1½	cups instant couscous
½	teaspoon salt
2¼	cups boiling water
¼	cup diced red onion
3	14-ounce cans artichoke hearts, rinsed, drained and quartered
½	cup chopped fresh basil
2	garlic cloves, minced
3	tomatoes, chopped
2	tablespoons extra-virgin or herb-flavored olive oil
2	tablespoons red wine vinegar
	Salt and pepper
1	avocado, diced

CAN A SALAD qualify as comfort food? It can when it is a luxuriously smooth combination of couscous, tomatoes, artichokes and avocado. This easy-to-prepare salad is an indulgence.

1. Combine the couscous, salt and boiling water in a large mixing bowl. Cover and let stand until the couscous is tender and the water is absorbed, about 10 minutes. Fluff with a fork. Cool to room temperature.

2. Add the onion, artichoke hearts, basil and garlic and toss lightly. (The salad can be held in the refrigerator for several hours at this point.)

3. Before serving, bring the salad to room temperature. Add the tomatoes, oil and vinegar and toss. Season with salt and pepper to taste. Add the avocado, gently toss again and serve.

Couscous Vegetable Salad
with Salsa Vinaigrette

Makes 4 to 6 servings

THIS IS ONE of my favorite throw-together salads—a boldly seasoned combination of couscous, kidney beans, tomatoes, cucumbers, parsley and cilantro, dressed with a combination of salsa, oil and lemon juice. Take it to picnics or potlucks.

2	cups instant couscous
1	teaspoon salt
3	cups boiling water
1	English cucumber, diced
½	cup chopped scallions or diced sweet or red onion
1	15-ounce can kidney beans, rinsed and drained
1	cup fresh or frozen peas
1	cup chopped fresh parsley
¼	cup chopped fresh cilantro
2	large tomatoes, peeled and diced
3	tablespoons extra-virgin olive oil
	Juice of 1-2 lemons
¾-1	cup prepared salsa
	Salt and pepper

1. Combine the couscous, salt and boiling water in a large mixing bowl. Cover and let stand until the couscous is tender and the water is absorbed, about 10 minutes. Fluff with a fork. Cool to room temperature.

2. Add the cucumber, scallions or onion, beans, peas, parsley and cilantro; toss. (The salad can be held in the refrigerator for several hours.)

3. Before serving, bring to room temperature. Add the tomatoes; toss. Combine the oil, 2 tablespoons lemon juice and salsa in a small bowl. Toss with the salad. Season with salt, pepper and lemon juice to taste and serve.

Warm Lentil Salad *with* Goat Cheese *and* Roasted Onions

1	pound white pearl onions
3	tablespoons extra-virgin olive oil
½	teaspoon dried thyme
1½	cups dried French green lentils
2	tablespoons plus 1 teaspoon balsamic vinegar
4	ounces mild goat cheese, such as Montrachet, crumbled
	Salt and pepper
8	cups torn mixed salad greens

1. Preheat the oven to 400°F. Combine the onions, 2 tablespoons of the oil and thyme in a roasting pan. Roast until lightly browned, 30 to 35 minutes.

2. Meanwhile, boil the lentils in plenty of salted water in a medium saucepan until tender but not mushy, about 25 minutes. Drain and transfer to a large mixing bowl.

3. Gently mix the roasted onions into the lentils. Add 2 tablespoons of the balsamic vinegar and three-quarters of the goat cheese. Season with salt and pepper to taste. Toss gently to mix.

4. Toss the greens with the remaining 1 tablespoon olive oil and 1 teaspoon balsamic vinegar. Arrange them on individual dinner plates or a serving platter. Spoon the lentil mixture on top. Garnish with the remaining goat cheese and serve.

Makes 4 servings

TANGY GOAT CHEESE and sweet roasted onions prove to be a wonderful foil for the nutty flavor of lentils. French green lentils are the variety of choice for this simple combination, because they hold their shape so well. Look for them at food co-ops and specialty food stores. Don't substitute ordinary brown lentils.

Likewise, pearl onions are preferable because of their shape. Since they are not always available, you can substitute white boiling onions (quartered or cut into eighths, if large).

Southwestern Rice and Bean Salad

**Makes
4 servings**

THE EARTHY FLAVORS of the black beans and green olives are well matched by the lime juice and cilantro in this colorful salad. A guaranteed crowd-pleaser, it is easy to transport. In the summer, garnish it with fresh tomato wedges to add even more color.

About 3 cups cooked white or brown rice
   (from 1 cup uncooked)
2 cups fresh or frozen corn kernels
1 15-ounce can black beans, rinsed and drained
1 red bell pepper, finely diced
1 green bell pepper, finely diced
½ cup chopped scallions
½ cup chopped fresh cilantro
2 tablespoons chopped green pimiento-stuffed olives
2 tablespoons extra-virgin olive oil
3 tablespoons fresh lime juice
   Salt and pepper
   Tomato wedges for garnish (optional)

1. Combine the rice, corn, beans, peppers, scallions, cilantro and olives in a large salad bowl. Toss to mix.

2. Add the oil and lime juice and toss to mix. Season to taste with salt and pepper. Serve at once, or refrigerate for a few hours, then bring to room temperature before serving. Garnish with tomato wedges, if desired.

Jamaican-Style Rice and Pea Salad

2 cups uncooked long-grain white rice

2 cups "light" coconut milk

2 cups water

2 15-ounce cans red kidney beans, rinsed and drained

4 scallions, chopped

2 carrots, grated

1 fresh hot green pepper, diced

2 tablespoons chopped fresh cilantro

1½ teaspoons dried thyme

2 tablespoons extra-virgin olive oil

6 tablespoons white wine vinegar

Salt and pepper

Makes 4 servings

THE CLASSIC DISH of coconut-flavored rice and red beans, known in Jamaica as "rice and peas," inspired this satisfying salad of multiple flavors and textures. The combination of coconut milk, cilantro, scallions, hot pepper and thyme has a tropical taste.

Unsweetened coconut milk can be found wherever Caribbean or Asian foods are sold. For a version that is lighter in fat and calories, look for Thai Kitchen's "lite" coconut milk, which is the unsweetened milk after the heavier solids are skimmed off.

1. Wash the rice in several changes of water until the water runs clear. Drain well. Combine the rice with the coconut milk and the 2 cups water in a medium saucepan. Cover, bring to a boil, reduce the heat to low and simmer gently until the rice is tender and all the liquid is absorbed, 12 to 15 minutes. Fluff with a fork and set aside to cool.

2. Transfer the cooled rice to a large salad bowl. Add the beans, scallions, carrots, hot pepper, cilantro and thyme; toss. (The salad can be held in the refrigerator for several hours at this point.)

3. Before serving, bring the salad to room temperature. Add the oil and vinegar, season with salt and pepper to taste and serve.

Curried Rice and Broccoli Salad with Mango Chutney Vinaigrette

**Makes
4 servings**

THIS IS A BEAUTIFUL salad of yellow rice, bright green broccoli and vivid red pepper. A sweet-sour vinaigrette made with mango chutney, lemon juice, mint and cilantro provides a tangy contrast to the curried rice. The salad survives well in the heat—an excellent choice for a picnic.

2	cups uncooked white rice
1	tablespoon peanut or canola oil
¼	cup minced onion
2	minced garlic cloves
1	tablespoon curry powder
1	tablespoon minced gingerroot
1	teaspoon salt
3½	cups water
1	pound broccoli, cut into small florets, stems diced
1	red bell pepper, diced
¼	cup unsweetened shredded coconut
1¼	cups Mango Chutney Vinaigrette (page 147)

1. Wash the rice in several changes of water until the water runs clear. Drain well.

2. In a medium saucepan, heat the oil over medium heat. Add the onion, garlic, curry powder, gingerroot and rice. Sauté until the rice appears dry, about 4 minutes. Add the salt and the 3½ cups water, cover, bring to a boil, reduce the heat to low and simmer gently until the rice is tender and the water is absorbed, about 15 minutes. Fluff with a fork and set aside to cool.

3. Meanwhile, blanch the broccoli in boiling water to cover for about 45 seconds. Plunge into cold water to stop the cooking; drain well.

4. In a large salad bowl, combine the cooled rice, broccoli, bell pepper and coconut. (The salad can be held in the refrigerator for several hours at this point.)

5. Before serving, bring the salad to room temperature. Pour the vinaigrette over it and toss well. Taste and adjust the seasonings before serving.

Wild Rice
and Wild Mushroom Salad

Makes
4 servings

M Y LOCAL FOOD co-op has such a lovely display of mushrooms each fall that it is impossible not to be inspired to cook with them. Of course, most of the mushrooms labeled "wild" are raised domestically, but they make up in flavor what they lack in authenticity.

1   red bell pepper
1   tablespoon extra-virgin olive oil or walnut oil
1   pound white mushrooms, sliced
1   pound wild mushrooms (chanterelles, morels, shiitakes, oyster mushrooms, cèpes), sliced
Salt and pepper
1   leek, quartered, well washed and sliced
About 3 cups cooked brown rice (from 1 cup uncooked)
About 1 cup cooked wild rice (from ⅓ cup uncooked)
½   cup chopped fresh parsley
2   tablespoons chopped fresh sage
Juice of 1-2 lemons

1. Roast the red pepper over an open flame or under a broiler, turning occasionally, until evenly charred. Place the charred pepper in a paper bag, seal the bag and place in the freezer for about 10 minutes to loosen the skin. Peel, remove seeds and chop. Set aside in a large salad bowl.

2. In a large nonstick skillet over high heat, heat the oil. Add half the white and wild mushrooms and sauté until well browned, about 10 minutes. Season with salt and pepper and add to the chopped pepper in the salad bowl. Repeat with the remaining mushrooms.

3. Add the leek to the skillet and sauté until limp and beginning to brown, about 5 minutes. Add to the salad bowl along with the brown rice, wild rice, parsley and sage. Toss well. (The salad can be held in the refrigerator for several hours at this point.)

4. Before serving, bring the salad to room temperature. Dress with 2 tablespoons of the lemon juice. Season to taste with salt and pepper, adding more lemon juice if needed, and serve at once.

BUY MUSHROOMS that are firm, not mushy or limp. Use as quickly as possible, but if you must hold them for a day or so, keep them in tightly sealed brown paper (not plastic) bags in the crisper drawer of the refrigerator.

Barley Broccoli Salad
with Roasted Garlic Vinaigrette

Makes 5 to 6 servings

NUTTY GRAINS of barley offer a fine alternative to rice in salads. Barley takes longer to cook than rice, but its chewy texture and slightly sweet flavor contrast nicely with the tender-crisp vegetables and the garlicky dressing. A loaf of rye bread or whole wheat goes well with this salad.

2 cups pearled barley
7 cups water
  Salt
1 pound broccoli crowns, cut into small florets, stems diced
8 scallions, diced
2 red bell peppers, diced
2 carrots, diced
1 cup chopped fresh basil
2 cups Roasted Garlic Vinaigrette (page 144)
  Fresh lemon juice (optional)
  Freshly ground pepper to taste

1. Place the barley in a strainer and set the strainer in a bowl. Run cold water through the barley, swishing with your hands, until the water runs clear. Drain well. Bring the 7 cups water to a boil in a large saucepan, add 1 teaspoon salt and the barley, cover, and return to a boil. Reduce the heat to low and simmer until the liquid is absorbed and the grains are just tender, about 30 minutes. Drain off any excess water. Fluff with a fork. Cool to room temperature.

2. Meanwhile, blanch the broccoli in boiling water to cover for 1 minute. Plunge into cold water to stop the cooking. Drain well.

3. In a large salad bowl, combine the barley with the broccoli, scallions, peppers, carrots and basil. Toss well. (The salad can be held in the refrigerator for several hours at this point.)

4. Before serving, bring the salad to room temperature. Pour the vinaigrette over it and toss again. Taste and add lemon juice, salt and pepper as needed and serve.

Chapter Three

From Sea *and* Stream

Mediterranean Seafood Salad

Makes

4 servings

SQUID IS THE STAR of this salad, with its distinctively briny flavor and slightly chewy character. The mussels, scallops and shrimp are cooked in the same broth, and with each step, taste intensifies.

A touch of wine, olive oil and fresh lemon juice marinates the seafood and creates a simple salad dressing. This elegant dish is perfect for a summer dinner party. Serve it with plenty of white wine and French bread.

	Salt
1½	pounds squid, cleaned and cut into ¾-inch rings and small pieces
2	pounds mussels in the shell
	About 1 cup dry white wine
1	pound bay or calico scallops
1	pound shrimp in the shell
2	tablespoons extra-virgin olive oil
2½	tablespoons fresh lemon juice or more to taste
1	cup chopped fresh parsley
10-12	cups torn mixed salad greens

1. Bring a medium saucepan full of lightly salted water to a boil. Add the squid, reduce the heat to low and simmer until tender, about 1 minute. Drain and set aside to cool.

2. Scrub the mussels, pull off their beards and wash in several changes of water. Discard any that do not close when tapped. Place about ¼ inch wine in a large, heavy-bottomed saucepan, add the mussels, cover, and bring to a boil. Steam for 3 to 10 minutes, until the shells open. Remove from the heat and discard any mussels that remain closed. Reserve the cooking liquid. When they are cool enough to handle, remove the mussels from the shells and set aside.

3. Strain the mussel-cooking liquid and return to the saucepan. Add the scallops and poach until tender, 3 to 5 minutes. Drain, reserving the cooking liquid.

4. Return the cooking liquid to the saucepan. Add the shrimp and additional boiling water if needed to cover and poach until they turn pink, about 3 minutes. When they are cool enough to handle, peel them. Reserve the cooking liquid.

5. Combine the cooled squid, mussels, scallops and shrimp in a large bowl. Pour the oil, 2½ tablespoons lemon juice and the reserved cooking liquid over them. Marinate in the refrigerator for about 1 hour before serving. Stir in the chopped parsley. Taste and season with salt and lemon juice as needed.

6. Arrange the greens on a large platter or individual plates. Spoon the seafood over them. Serve at once.

SQUID SOMETIMES presents a challenge for a cook because it becomes tough and rubbery if overcooked—which can happen in less than a minute. Then you must simmer it back to tenderness. Keep a careful eye on the clock, but if you lose track of the time, cook the squid for about 40 minutes more, or until it is tender again.

Paella Salad

**Makes
4 servings**

IN SPAIN, there are
hundreds of versions
of paella—that exquisite
combination of saffron-
scented rice with seafood
or meat. I took the same
flavors and ingredients and
united them with a light,
lemony dressing. The result
is an elegant and beautiful
salad, rich with smoky
turkey, sweet shrimp and
saffron. This is a wonderful
choice for a special-occasion
meal, especially because you
can make it early in the day.

2	cups uncooked long-grain white rice
3½	cups water
½	teaspoon salt
⅛	teaspoon crushed saffron
2	garlic cloves, minced
½	pound smoked turkey breast, diced (1¾ cups)
½	pound cooked, peeled small shrimp
1	red bell pepper, diced
1	cup fresh or frozen green peas
4	scallions, chopped
½	cup chopped fresh parsley
2	tablespoons extra-virgin olive oil
	Juice of 1 lemon
	Salt and pepper
	Watercress, cherry tomatoes,
	strips of red bell pepper (optional)

1. Wash the rice in several changes of water until the water runs clear.
Drain well.

2. In a medium saucepan, combine the rice, the 3½ cups water, salt, saffron and garlic over medium-high heat. Cover, bring to a boil, reduce the
heat to low and simmer until the rice is tender and all the water is absorbed, about 12 minutes. Spoon into a large salad bowl to cool.

3. When the rice is mostly cooled, add the turkey, shrimp, bell pepper, peas, scallions and parsley. (The salad can be refrigerated for several hours at this point.)

4. Before serving, bring the salad to room temperature. Add the oil and 2 tablespoons lemon juice. Taste and season with salt, pepper and more lemon juice as needed. Garnish as desired with sprigs of watercress, cherry tomatoes or strips of bell pepper and serve.

Warm Scallop Salad
with Citrus Vinaigrette

**Makes
4 servings**

In this salad, pan-seared scallops top warm greens dressed with a citrusy vinaigrette. The secret to perfectly sautéed scallops: Make sure they are well chilled and absolutely dry before adding them to the pan.

1½	pounds sea scallops, patted dry
	Salt and pepper
1	small zucchini, julienned
1	carrot, julienned
2	scallions, julienned
¾	cup defatted chicken broth
⅔	cup Citrus Vinaigrette (page 146)
10-12	cups torn mixed salad greens

1. Preheat a large nonstick sauté pan over medium-high heat. Spray lightly with nonstick cooking spray. Add half the scallops, sprinkle with salt and pepper and cook until browned on the bottom, 2 to 3 minutes. Turn and cook until browned on the other side and just cooked through, 1 to 2 minutes more. Transfer to a large plate. Spray the pan with more cooking spray and cook the remaining scallops; transfer to the plate.

2. Add the zucchini, carrot and scallions to the pan and sauté until barely tender-crisp, about 1 minute. Remove from the pan; transfer to another plate.

3. Add the broth to the pan. Bring to a boil and boil over high heat until reduced to about ¼ cup, about 5 minutes. Stir in the vinaigrette and remove from the heat.

4. Add any juices that have accumulated from the scallops to the warmed vinaigrette. In a large bowl, toss the greens with the vinaigrette. Season to taste with salt and pepper. Arrange the greens on individual serving plates. Top with the scallops, then garnish with the sautéed vegetables. Serve at once.

Shrimp *and* Avocado Salad *with* Cilantro-Lime Vinaigrette

**Makes
4 servings**

A Southwestern-style vinaigrette with cilantro and lime brings just the right flavor to this salad of shrimp, avocado, black beans, sweet and hot peppers and jicama. The baked tortilla chips add extra crunch. If you like, you can use them to scoop up every last bite.

1   pound medium shrimp in the shell
    (½ pound cooked, peeled)
1   15-ounce can black beans, rinsed and drained
1   avocado, diced
1   carrot, julienned
1   red bell pepper, julienned
1   green bell pepper, julienned
1   cup julienned jicama (optional)
½   English cucumber, julienned
½   cup julienned scallions
1   teaspoon minced fresh red or green hot pepper
    or more to taste

Cilantro-Lime Vinaigrette

3   tablespoons fresh lime juice
1   tablespoon white wine vinegar
2   garlic cloves, minced
¼   cup chopped fresh cilantro
2   tablespoons extra-virgin olive oil

    Salt and pepper
1-2 heads butter lettuce
6   ounces baked tortilla chips

1. If using shrimp in the shell, poach them in a medium pot in barely simmering water for 4 to 5 minutes, until pink and opaque. Drain; peel. Combine the shrimp, beans, avocado, carrot, bell peppers, jicama (if using), cucumber, scallions and hot pepper in a large bowl and toss lightly to mix.

2. To make the lime vinaigrette: In a small bowl, combine the lime juice, vinegar, garlic and cilantro. Whisk in the oil.

3. Pour the vinaigrette over the shrimp salad. Toss lightly to mix. Season with salt and pepper to taste.

4. Make a bed of lettuce on individual plates. Surround the lettuce with the chips. Heap the shrimp salad in the middle. Serve at once.

Vietnamese Shrimp and Vegetable Salad

**Makes
4 servings**

THIS IS A PERFECT warm-weather salad—a snappy mix of shrimp, carrots, cucumber and daikon, a giant white radish. The salad requires almost no cooking (none if you buy your shrimp cooked), and it is light, yet satisfying. The dressing, a classic Vietnamese dipping sauce, contains no oil—just fish sauce, white vinegar, sugar and garlic.

3 cups julienned carrots
3 cups julienned English cucumber
2 cups julienned peeled daikon
3 teaspoons salt

Dressing
9 tablespoons fish sauce
9 tablespoons white vinegar
6 tablespoons sugar
2 teaspoons finely chopped garlic

1 pound cooked, peeled medium or large shrimp
6-8 cups finely shredded romaine lettuce
Chopped fresh cilantro

1. Combine the carrots, cucumber and daikon with the salt in a medium bowl and let stand for 10 minutes. Rinse the salt off with cold running water and drain well. Set aside.

2. To make the dressing: Combine the fish sauce, vinegar, sugar and garlic in a small bowl and stir until the sugar dissolves.

3. In a large bowl, combine the shrimp and vegetables with two-thirds of the dressing. Toss well. (The salad can be held in the refrigerator for several hours at this point.)

4. Before serving, bring the salad to room temperature. Arrange the lettuce on individual dinner plates or a large serving platter. Spoon the salad on top. Sprinkle with the cilantro. Pass the remaining dressing at the table.

YOU CAN BUY DAIKON wherever Asian foods are sold—and it is often found in supermarkets as well. Daikon is usually peeled before it is sliced. You won't use a whole one in a single sitting, so store whatever you have left, tightly wrapped, in the crisper drawer of the refrigerator for a week or more.

ON A HOT DAY, I have no problem with buying already-cooked shrimp at the fish store. But if you want to cook them yourself, buy 2 pounds medium or large shrimp in the shell and poach them in gently boiling water for 4 to 5 minutes, until pink and opaque throughout. Peel after cooking—cooking them in the shell intensifies their flavor.

Chinese Shrimp and Vegetable Salad

**Makes
4 servings**

The addition of shrimp makes this spinach salad festive, while crisp Asian vegetables and a soy-sesame dressing give it a Chinese touch.

Salad

1½ pounds medium shrimp in the shell
    (¾ pound cooked, peeled)
8 cups torn spinach, tough stems removed
2 cups finely sliced bok choy
1 cup bean sprouts
4 scallions, chopped

Dressing

3 tablespoons soy sauce
2 tablespoons rice wine vinegar
2 teaspoons sugar
1 tablespoon sesame oil
1 tablespoon water

1 tablespoon finely chopped peanuts (optional)

1. To make the salad: If using shrimp in the shell, poach them in a medium pot in barely simmering water for 4 to 5 minutes, until pink and opaque. Drain. Peel, then chill.

2. Combine the spinach, bok choy, bean sprouts, scallions and shrimp in a large salad bowl.

3. To make the dressing: Combine the soy sauce, vinegar, sugar, sesame oil and water in a small bowl and whisk until well blended. (The salad and dressing can be refrigerated in separate containers for several hours at this point.)

4. Just before serving, pour the dressing over the salad and toss well. Garnish with the chopped peanuts, if desired, and serve.

Shrimp *and* Noodle Salad *with* Soy-Chili Vinaigrette

**Makes
4 servings**

A SPICY combination of noodles, shrimp and Chinese vegetables is dressed in a delightfully bold sauce flavored with soy and chilies. The heat comes from a jar of chili paste with garlic, which is readily found wherever Asian foods are sold. There's just one problem with quantifying the amount to use: The chili paste loses potency over time. With a freshly opened jar, ½ teaspoon provides enough zing for my family. A month later, I need 2 teaspoons. Be sure to taste the salad before serving.

1	pound fresh Chinese noodles or ¾ pound dried linguine
1	tablespoon sesame oil
½	pound cooked, peeled small shrimp
½	pound (2 cups) snow peas, trimmed
6	scallions, cut into 2-inch lengths
1	15-ounce can baby corn, rinsed, drained and quartered
1	carrot, julienned

Soy-Chili Vinaigrette

¼	cup soy sauce
¼	cup defatted chicken broth
3	tablespoons rice wine vinegar
2	teaspoons sugar
½-3	teaspoons chili paste with garlic or more to taste
1	garlic clove, minced
1	teaspoon sesame oil

1. Cook the noodles in a large pot in plenty of boiling, salted water until tender but firm to the bite, 2 to 3 minutes for fresh noodles, 7 to 9 minutes for dried. Drain. Rinse briefly with cold running water. Drain well. Toss with the sesame oil.

2. In a large salad bowl, combine the noodles with the shrimp, snow peas, scallions, corn and carrot.

3. To make the vinaigrette: Combine the soy sauce, broth, vinegar, sugar, ½ teaspoon of the chili paste, garlic and sesame oil in a small bowl and blend well. Taste by dipping a noodle into the vinaigrette; add more chili paste as needed. (The salad and vinaigrette can be refrigerated in separate containers for several hours at this point.)

4. Before serving, bring to room temperature. Toss the salad with the vinaigrette and serve.

Japanese-Style Rice Salad with Shrimp

Makes 4 to 6 servings

THE JAPANESE present their food in serving dishes of all shapes and styles. This beautiful salad deserves Japanese-style special treatment, and the dressed rice can be easily molded to make that possible. Consider serving the salad on a flat plate (a rectangular one would be perfect) with the rice molded in a bowl and then inverted onto the plate and the shrimp arranged around the edges. Or mound the rice in a bowl, and hang the large shrimp over the rim.

2 pounds large shrimp in the shell (1 pound cooked, peeled)
12 dried shiitake mushrooms
2 tablespoons mirin (sweet Japanese rice wine)
2 tablespoons tamari
About 4 cups cooked white or brown rice, cooled (from 1¼ cups uncooked)
1½ cups bean sprouts
1 cup snow peas or sugar snap peas, trimmed
½ cup grated peeled daikon (giant white radish)
1 small carrot, grated
4 scallions, chopped
2 tablespoons chopped fresh cilantro

Dressing
3 tablespoons tamari
3 tablespoons rice wine vinegar
1 tablespoon mirin (sweet Japanese rice wine)
1 tablespoon sugar
1 1-inch piece gingerroot, minced
1 garlic clove, minced
1 tablespoon sesame oil

1. If using shrimp in the shell, poach them in a medium pot in barely simmering water for 4 to 5 minutes, until pink and opaque. Drain. Peel, then chill.

2. Place the mushrooms with the mirin and tamari in a small bowl. Add boiling water to cover. Set aside to soften for at least 20 minutes.

3. Combine the cooled rice with the vegetables and cilantro in a large bowl. When the mushrooms are soft, remove and discard the stems and slice the caps. Add to the rice salad and toss to mix.

4. To make the dressing: Combine the tamari, rice wine vinegar, mirin, sugar, ginger and garlic in a small bowl; whisk in the sesame oil.

5. Just before serving, pour the dressing over the rice salad; toss lightly. Transfer to individual bowls or a large platter, arranging the shrimp around the edges. Serve at once.

HOWEVER YOU SERVE it, you are sure to enjoy the simple combination of rice and vegetables, dressed lightly with ginger, tamari and cilantro.

Gingered Rice *and* Shrimp Salad

**Makes
4 servings**

OOKING RICE with ginger permeates it with a delicate flavor. The rice is then combined with vegetables and shrimp and tossed with a light tamari-based dressing.

2 pounds large shrimp in the shell
    (1 pound cooked, peeled)
2 cups uncooked white rice
3½ cups water
1 1-inch piece gingerroot, sliced,
    plus a 1-inch piece, minced
2 cups chopped spinach or watercress, tough
    stems removed
1 cup grated peeled daikon (giant white radish)
1 carrot, grated
4 scallions, chopped
½ cup Japanese Tamari-Sesame Dressing (page 150)

1. If using shrimp in the shell, poach them in a medium saucepan in barely simmering water for 4 to 5 minutes, until pink and opaque. Drain. Peel, then chill.

2. Wash the rice in several changes of water until the water runs clear. Drain well.

3. In a medium saucepan, combine the rice with the 3½ cups water and sliced gingerroot. Cover, bring to a boil, reduce the heat to low and simmer until the rice is tender and all the water is absorbed, about 12 minutes. Fluff with a fork. Discard the ginger. Set the rice aside to cool.

4. Combine the cooled rice with the shrimp and spinach or watercress, daikon, carrot and scallions in a large bowl. Add the minced ginger to the dressing. (The salad and dressing can be refrigerated in separate containers for up to 1 day at this point.)

5. Before serving, bring the salad and dressing to room temperature. Pour the dressing over the salad, toss lightly and serve.

Shrimp, White Bean and Arugula Salad

**Makes
4 servings**

THIS SALAD is a winning mix of flavors: briny shrimp, peppery arugula and nutty roasted garlic.

1½   pounds medium shrimp in the shell
      (¾ pound cooked, peeled)
12   cups torn arugula
4   medium tomatoes, cut into wedges
1   19-ounce can cannellini beans, rinsed and drained
¾   cup Roasted Garlic Vinaigrette (page 144)
½   cup thinly sliced Vidalia or similar sweet onion
2   teaspoons capers, drained

1. If using shrimp in the shell, poach them in a medium saucepan in barely simmering water for 4 to 5 minutes, until pink and opaque. Drain. Peel, then chill.

2. Just before serving, place a bed of arugula on individual plates. Arrange the tomato wedges around the outside. Spoon the beans onto the center of the greens. Drizzle with half the vinaigrette. Arrange the shrimp on top of the beans, then top with the onion and capers. Drizzle with the remaining vinaigrette and serve.

Tuscany Tuna Salad
with White Beans

1	6½-to-7-ounce can water-packed tuna, drained and flaked
4	scallions, chopped
3	garlic cloves, minced
½	cup chopped fresh basil
2	tablespoons capers, drained
4	tablespoons red wine vinegar
1	tablespoon extra-virgin olive oil or herb-flavored oil
2	tablespoons defatted chicken broth
1	15-ounce can cannellini beans, rinsed and drained
	Salt and pepper
12	cups torn mixed salad greens
4	Italian plum tomatoes, chopped

**Makes
4 servings**

FOR A DINNER you can toss together in less than 20 minutes, nothing beats this summery tuna salad. It needs only a jug of wine and a loaf of bread to complete it. If you can also provide a summer breeze, a lovely view from a shaded porch and the scent of flowers in the air, so much the better. Sweet vine-ripened tomatoes and fresh basil are a must to properly complement the briny tuna and capers and the earthy beans.

1. In a large salad bowl, combine the tuna, scallions, garlic, basil, capers, vinegar, oil and broth. Toss to mix. Gently fold in the beans. Season with salt and pepper to taste. (The salad can be refrigerated for up to 4 hours at this point.)

2. Just before serving, add the greens and the tomatoes to the tuna mixture, toss and serve.

Shells *with* Mussels *in* Creamy Mustard-Thyme Sauce

Makes 4 to 6 servings

BUTTERMILK provides the creamy background for the mustard-thyme dressing, which is sensational with plump, freshly cooked mussels.

1   pound dried small pasta shells

1   tablespoon extra-virgin olive oil

1   red bell pepper, diced

1   cup fresh or frozen green peas

1   cup chopped fresh watercress, tough stems removed

½   cup chopped fresh parsley

4   pounds mussels in the shell, scrubbed and debearded

¾   cup dry white wine

4   garlic cloves, minced

2   shallots, minced

Creamy Mustard-Thyme Sauce

¾   cup nonfat buttermilk

¼   cup reduced-fat mayonnaise

2   tablespoons Dijon-style mustard

2   tablespoons white wine vinegar

1½   tablespoons honey

2   shallots, minced

1   tablespoon fresh thyme or 1 teaspoon dried

Salt and pepper

Sprigs of fresh thyme for garnish (optional)

1. Cook the pasta in a large pot in plenty of boiling, salted water until tender but firm to the bite, 10 to 13 minutes. Drain. Rinse lightly. Transfer to a large salad bowl and toss with the oil. Add the red pepper, peas, watercress and parsley. Set aside.

2. In a large pot, combine the mussels, wine, garlic and shallots. Cover and steam over high heat, shaking the pot frequently, until the mussels open, about 10 minutes. Discard any that remain closed. Discard the broth, or strain and reserve for another use. Shell the mussels and set aside.

3. To make the mustard sauce: Combine all the ingredients in a blender and process until smooth. (The pasta salad, the shelled mussels and the sauce can be refrigerated in separate containers for several hours at this point.)

4. Just before serving, add the mussels to the pasta salad. Add the sauce and toss to combine. Taste and add salt and pepper as needed. If desired, garnish with the sprigs of thyme. Serve chilled or at room temperature.

Creamy Crab and Asparagus Salad

**Makes
4 servings**

When asparagus is in season, celebrate with a supper of tender-crisp spears topped with a creamy crab salad.

1½   pounds asparagus, trimmed
1   pound crabmeat, picked over
1   cup chopped celery
1   carrot, grated
2   scallions, finely chopped
1   tablespoon finely chopped fresh dill
1   teaspoon finely grated lemon zest
1   teaspoon capers, drained
1   cup nonfat buttermilk
½   cup reduced-fat mayonnaise
¼   cup fresh lemon juice
     Salt and pepper to taste
     Dill sprigs for garnish (optional)

1. Steam the asparagus over boiling water until just tender, 3 to 4 minutes. Drain, plunge into cold water to stop the cooking; drain again. Set aside.

2. Combine the remaining ingredients in a medium bowl. Taste and adjust the seasonings, adding salt and pepper as needed.

3. Arrange the asparagus on individual serving plates. Top with the crab salad. Garnish with sprigs of fresh dill, if you like, and serve.

Thai-Style Crab *and* Asparagus Salad

1½   pounds asparagus, trimmed and
        roll-cut into 1½-inch lengths
3   1.75-ounce packages cellophane noodles
1   pound crabmeat, picked over
1   carrot, grated
¼   cup chopped fresh mint
¼   cup chopped fresh cilantro
2   tablespoons minced shallots
1-2   fresh hot green peppers, finely shredded
2   teaspoons minced garlic
2   teaspoons minced peeled gingerroot
¼   cup fresh lime juice
3   tablespoons fish sauce
2   tablespoons sugar

**Makes
4 servings**

MINT, LIME AND cilantro form a trio of flavors in this light, refreshing salad. The dressing is an oil-free combination of fish sauce, lime juice and sugar. The exotic ingredients—cellophane (bean thread) noodles and fish sauce—can be found with Asian foods. If asparagus isn't in season, substitute another vegetable, such as green beans.

To roll-cut the asparagus, slice off one end on the diagonal. Rotate the spear a quarter turn and cut again at the same angle.

1. Steam the asparagus over boiling water until just tender, 3 to 4 minutes. Drain, plunge into cold water to stop the cooking; drain. Set aside.

2. Soak the noodles in hot water to cover for about 5 minutes. Drain.

3. Combine the crab, carrot, mint, cilantro, shallots, peppers, garlic and ginger in a medium mixing bowl. In a small bowl, combine the lime juice, fish sauce and sugar, stirring to dissolve the sugar. Add to the salad; toss.

4. Line a platter or individual plates with the noodles. Top with the asparagus, then the crabmeat salad and serve.

Mediterranean Tuna Vegetable Salad

**Makes
4 servings**

Tuna from a can, when anointed with extra-virgin olive oil, red wine vinegar and capers, makes a quick-to-prepare salad supper. I like to combine the tuna with an assortment of crisp vegetables and toss it all together with mixed greens. Hold the mayo, please!

1	cup green beans, cut into 1½-inch pieces
1	15-ounce can chickpeas, rinsed and drained
1	14-ounce can artichoke hearts, rinsed, drained and quartered
1	carrot, julienned
½	green bell pepper, thinly sliced
½	cup brined Greek olives, pitted, if desired
¼	cup diced red onion
1-2	tablespoons capers, drained
¼	cup red wine vinegar
¼	cup defatted chicken broth
¼	cup chopped fresh basil
4	garlic cloves, minced
1	tablespoon extra-virgin olive oil
1	6½ -to-7-ounce can water-packed tuna, drained and flaked
4	plum tomatoes, diced
	Salt and pepper
12	cups torn mixed salad greens

1. In a small saucepan, blanch the green beans in water to cover for 45 seconds; they will be crunchy and bright green. Plunge into cold water to stop the cooking; drain.

2. In a large salad bowl, combine the beans, chickpeas, artichoke hearts, carrot, green pepper, olives, onion and capers.

3. In a small bowl, whisk together the vinegar, broth, basil, garlic and oil. Pour over the vegetables. If you have the time, set the salad aside for at least 30 minutes at room temperature or for up to 8 hours in the refrigerator, tossing occasionally, to allow the flavors to develop.

4. Just before serving, add the tuna and tomatoes to the salad and toss well. Season with salt and pepper to taste. Add the greens and toss again. Taste and adjust the seasonings, adding salt and pepper as needed, and serve.

Poached Salmon Salad
with Herbed Cucumber Sauce

**Makes
4 servings**

I LOVE TO SERVE this salad as a special-occasion springtime meal. It is easily put together just before serving, or you can make up the components early in the day and assemble the plates at the last minute.

Whatever your time frame, guests always perk up at the combination of moist, fresh salmon on a bed of peppery watercress and asparagus, napped with a light sauce of cucumber, tarragon or dill and yogurt.

4	6-ounce salmon fillets, skin and bones removed
1½	quarts water
2	heaping tablespoons salt
1	pound asparagus, trimmed

Herbed Cucumber Sauce

1½	cups plain nonfat yogurt
1	English cucumber, finely chopped
2	scallions, chopped
¼	cup chopped fresh parsley
1	tablespoon chopped fresh tarragon or dill
	Salt and pepper to taste
2	bunches watercress, tough stems removed

1. Place the salmon fillets in a pot large enough to hold them and cover with cold water. Add the salt and bring just to a boil. Turn off the heat and let stand until the fish is completely done, about 8 minutes. Remove the fish from the water and let cool to room temperature. (If desired, the fish can be refrigerated for several hours before proceeding with the recipe. Bring the fish to room temperature before serving.)

2. Steam the asparagus over boiling water until barely tender, 3 to 4 minutes. Plunge immediately into cold water to stop the cooking, and drain well.

3. To make the sauce: In a small bowl, stir together the yogurt, cucumber, scallions, parsley and tarragon or dill. Taste and adjust the seasonings, adding salt and pepper as needed.

4. Arrange the watercress on individual plates. Place the salmon and asparagus on the watercress. Pour a saddle of cucumber sauce over each fillet and pass the remaining sauce at the table.

Warm Asparagus and New Potato Salad with Pan-Seared Trout

**Makes
4 servings**

ALTHOUGH IT HAS become a year-round item in the supermarket, nothing beats the fresh taste of local asparagus each spring. Here the spears are paired with new potatoes in a warm salad lightly dressed with balsamic vinegar, shallots and thyme. Pan-seared trout is a perfect complement.

1½ pounds new potatoes, halved, quartered
    or cut into eighths, depending on size (do not peel)
1 pound asparagus, trimmed and cut into 2-inch lengths
2 tablespoons extra-virgin olive oil
1 shallot, minced
2 teaspoons chopped fresh thyme or 1 teaspoon dried
½ cup defatted chicken broth
1 tablespoon balsamic vinegar
Salt and pepper
4 4-to-5-ounce trout fillets
12 cups torn mixed salad greens

1. In a medium saucepan, bring the potatoes to a boil in salted water to cover. Cover the pan and boil gently until just tender, about 8 minutes. Remove from the heat and set aside.

2. Steam the asparagus over boiling water until just tender, 3 to 4 minutes. Remove from the heat, plunge into cold water to stop the cooking, and drain well.

3. Heat 1 tablespoon of the oil in a large skillet. Add the shallot and sauté until limp, about 2 minutes. Add the asparagus, potatoes and thyme and toss to coat with the oil. Add the broth and vinegar. Bring to a boil. Transfer to a large bowl and season to taste with salt and pepper.

4. Heat 1½ teaspoons of the oil in the skillet. Add 2 of the fillets in a single layer and cook, turning once, until golden brown on both sides, about 4 minutes total. Transfer to a plate. Repeat, using the remaining 1½ teaspoons oil and the remaining 2 fillets.

5. Arrange the salad greens on individual plates. Place the fillets on top of the greens. Spoon the asparagus salad around the edges. Combine any pan juices with any dressing remaining in the bowl that held the asparagus salad, drizzle over the fillets and serve at once.

Wasabi-Grilled Swordfish
with Soy-Sesame Spinach Salad

**Makes
4 servings**

WASABI IS THE
Japanese version
of horseradish, a sharply
pungent, green-colored
condiment that is usually
bought in powdered form
from Asian or health food
stores and mixed with water
just before serving. The
wasabi adds a gentle bite
to the meaty swordfish,
which sits on a bed of
spinach flavored with a light
sesame-and-soy dressing.

1	tablespoon tamari
1	tablespoon fresh lemon juice
1-1¼	pounds swordfish, cut into 4 steaks
1½	pounds fresh spinach, tough stems removed
1	cup grated carrot
½	cup Japanese Tamari-Sesame Dressing (page 150)
1	tablespoon wasabi powder, mixed with 1 tablespoon water
1	tablespoon sesame seeds, toasted (see page 46, step 2)

1. Combine the tamari and lemon juice and brush on the swordfish. Set aside while you prepare a hot fire in a charcoal or gas grill, with the rack set 3 to 4 inches above the coals.

2. Plunge the spinach into boiling water to wilt for about 30 seconds. Drain and plunge into ice-cold water to stop the cooking. Drain well and squeeze dry with your hands. Place in a medium bowl and combine with the carrot. Add the dressing and toss lightly.

3. Brush the wasabi paste on the fish. When the coals are hot, grill until just done, turning once, about 4 minutes per side.

4. Arrange the spinach in a ring around a platter or on individual plates. Sprinkle with the sesame seeds. Place the fish in the center of the platter or plates. Serve at once.

Smoked Trout Salad

Herb Sauce

1 cup chopped watercress, tough stems removed
2 shallots, chopped
Juice of ½ lemon
1 tablespoon capers, drained
1 tablespoon extra-virgin olive oil
1 cup fat-free sour cream
Salt and pepper

Salad

12 cups torn mixed salad greens
1 English cucumber, sliced
1 pint cherry tomatoes, halved
12 radishes, sliced
4 3-ounce smoked trout fillets, sliced into bite-size pieces
4 slices Vidalia or other sweet onion, separated into rings
Capers

**Makes
4 servings**

A CREAMY watercress-based sauce sets off the rich, slightly oily smoked fish. Add some greens, cucumbers and tomatoes, and you have a delicious dinner. Smoked bluefish or mackerel can replace the trout. Rye bread or pumpernickel goes well with this salad.

1. To make the sauce: Combine the watercress, shallots, lemon juice, capers and oil in a food processor. Process until finely chopped. Transfer to a small bowl and stir in the sour cream. Season with salt and pepper to taste. Set aside for at least 30 minutes to allow the flavors to develop.

2. To assemble the salad: Place a bed of mixed greens on individual plates. Arrange the vegetables on top. Top with the trout, spooning a little sauce over it. Scatter additional capers on top and serve. Pass the remaining sauce at the table.

Smoked Bluefish *and* Potato Salad

**Makes
4 servings**

THE FLAVOR of smoked fish transforms the creamy potato salad into a delicious light supper, especially when served with an Old World rye or pumpernickel bread. The dish also makes a delightful addition to a brunch. If smoked bluefish isn't available, substitute any other smoked fish.

6 medium-size red potatoes (1½-1¾ pounds),
   sliced into wedges (do not peel)
1 cup fresh or frozen peas
   or 2 cups snap peas or snow peas
1 cup sliced radishes
2 scallions, chopped
2 tablespoons minced fresh dill or 1 tablespoon dried
2 tablespoons extra-virgin olive oil
¼ cup fresh lemon juice
1 cup nonfat buttermilk
½ pound smoked bluefish, flaked
1 teaspoon capers, drained
   Salt and pepper
12 cups torn mixed salad greens
   (watercress, arugula,
   chicory, endive)
   Sliced radishes, lemon wedges,
   dill sprigs (optional)

1. In a medium saucepan, bring the potatoes to a boil in salted water to cover. Cover the pan and boil gently until just tender, about 8 minutes. Remove from the heat, plunge into cold water to stop the cooking, and drain well.

2. In a large mixing bowl, combine the potatoes, peas, radishes, scallions and dill. Add the oil and lemon juice and toss well. Add the buttermilk, fish and capers and toss thoroughly but gently. Taste and adjust the seasonings, adding salt, plenty of pepper and more dill as needed. If possible, chill for at least 1 hour.

3. Make a bed of greens on a platter or individual plates. Spoon the salad over the greens. Garnish with radishes, lemon wedges or dill sprigs, as desired, and serve.

Chapter Four

Birds *of* Many Flavors

Grilled Chicken Caesar Salad

**Makes
4 servings**

I THINK TRADITIONAL Caesar salads are best enjoyed at a bistro where wine and conversation can fill you up. For dinner, the addition of chicken or meat seems necessary.

This version is both satisfying and light. Good wine and conversations are not essential, but would certainly do no harm!

½   pound loaf French or Italian bread
1   pound boneless, skinless chicken breast
2   garlic cloves, minced
1   teaspoon fresh or dried rosemary
16   cups torn romaine lettuce
1½   cups Caesar Salad Dressing (page 149) or Roasted Garlic
       Vinaigrette (page 144; double the recipe)
¼   cup freshly grated Parmesan cheese
       Freshly ground pepper

1. Prepare a medium-hot fire in a charcoal or gas grill, with the rack set 3 to 4 inches above the coals.

2. Meanwhile, make the croutons: Lightly spray a baking sheet with olive-oil nonstick cooking spray. Cut the bread into 1-inch cubes. Arrange on the baking sheet and spray lightly with the cooking spray. Broil until golden brown, flipping once, 2 to 3 minutes per side.

3. To grill the chicken, lightly spray with olive-oil nonstick cooking spray. Combine the garlic and rosemary and rub on the meat. When the coals are medium-hot, grill the chicken for about 7 minutes per side, or until firm and white throughout. Set aside to cool.

4. Combine the lettuce and croutons in a large salad bowl. Cut the chicken into 1-inch cubes and add to the bowl. Pour on the dressing or vinaigrette; toss well. Sprinkle with the Parmesan and grind on some pepper, toss and serve.

Asian Shredded Chicken *and* Spinach Salad

8   cups torn spinach, tough stems removed
4   cups sliced napa cabbage or bok choy
2   cups bean sprouts
1   cup julienned peeled daikon (giant white radish)
1   cup julienned carrot
6   scallions, julienned
2   cups shredded cooked chicken
⅔   cup Lemon-Soy Dressing (page 151)

1. Combine the spinach, cabbage or bok choy, bean sprouts, daikon, carrot, scallions and chicken in a large salad bowl and toss to mix.

2. Just before serving, add the dressing, toss again and serve.

**Makes
4 servings**

THE LEMON-SOY Dressing that complements this spinach salad is one of my house specialties; I always keep it on hand in the refrigerator. You can easily vary the vegetables here, or substitute turkey or cooked shrimp for the chicken. A sprinkling of roasted peanuts makes a tasty garnish.

Grilled Chicken *with* Smoky Corn *and* Pepper Salad

**Makes
4 servings**

DURING SUMMER, a salad of roasted corn and peppers accented with cilantro and lime juice is a fine way to feast. Out of season, frozen corn, with the addition of a touch of sugar, will do the trick. Chipotles en adobo—a puree of smoke-dried jalapeños—does a marvelous job of infusing any dish with smoky flavor. This ingredient gives a barbecue flavor when the grill is buried beneath several feet of snow.

6   ears fresh corn (3 cups of kernels)
2   tablespoons fresh lime juice
1   teaspoon ground cumin
    Salt and pepper to taste
4   boneless, skinless chicken breast halves (about 1 pound)
1   red bell pepper, halved and seeded
1   green bell pepper, halved and seeded
1   tomato, diced
¼   cup diced red onion
¼   cup chopped fresh cilantro or basil
¼   cup chopped fresh parsley
1   tablespoon sugar (optional; not needed if the corn is sweet and fresh)

Chipotle-Lime Dressing

1   tablespoon olive oil
2   tablespoons fresh lime juice
1   teaspoon honey
1   teaspoon chipotles en adobo or more to taste
    Salt and pepper

8   cups torn mixed salad greens

1. If using ears of corn, soak them (still in the husks) in water to cover at least 1 hour before you plan to serve the salad.

2. In a shallow glass or nonreactive baking dish, combine the lime juice, cumin, salt and pepper. Add the chicken, turning to coat well with the marinade. Set aside to marinate while you prepare the grill.

3. Prepare a medium-hot fire in a charcoal or gas grill, with the rack set 3 to 4 inches above the coals. When the coals are medium-hot, grill the corn until the kernels are lightly toasted, 15 to 20 minutes. Set aside. Spray the peppers with nonstick cooking spray. Grill until lightly charred, turning occasionally, about 5 minutes. Set aside.

4. Grill the chicken over medium-hot coals until done, about 15 minutes, turning three or four times during the cooking. The chicken should be firm and white throughout. Set aside.

5. Remove the corn kernels from the cobs with a sharp knife. Dice the peppers. In a large bowl, combine the corn and peppers with the tomato, red onion, cilantro or basil and parsley. Add the sugar, if using.

6. To make the dressing: Mix all the ingredients in a small bowl. Add to the corn salad and toss. Season with salt and pepper.

7. To serve, place a bed of mixed greens on individual plates. Top each plate with one-fourth of the corn salad. Slice each chicken breast and lay the slices over the corn salad. Serve at once. For those who love hot foods, pass the chipotles en adobo at the table.

CHIPOTLES EN ADOBO is found in specialty stores where Mexican foods are carried. (For a good mail-order source, see page 45.)

Chicken Salad
with Dilled Mayonnaise

**Makes
4 servings**

IN THIS VARIATION on the familiar chicken salad, peppery watercress adds snap to the dill in the dressing. For a light summer meal, serve the salad on a bed of greens. It makes an equally good— and low-fat—filling for sandwiches.

1¼   pounds boneless, skinless chicken breast

Dilled Mayonnaise

2   cups chopped watercress, tough stems removed
4   garlic cloves, chopped
2   shallots, chopped
   Juice of ½ lemon
3   tablespoons chopped fresh dill
1   tablespoon extra-virgin olive oil
⅓   cup fat-free mayonnaise
⅓   cup plain low-fat yogurt
   Salt and pepper

1   red bell pepper, cubed
8   cups torn mixed salad greens
1   pint cherry tomatoes, halved if large

1. Place the chicken in a medium saucepan and cover with water. Bring just to a boil, reduce the heat to low and poach the chicken until white and firm throughout, about 15 minutes. Cool in the cooking liquid.

2. To make the dilled mayonnaise: Combine the watercress, garlic, shallots, lemon juice, dill and oil in a food processor and process until finely chopped. Stir in the mayonnaise and yogurt. Season with salt and pepper to taste.

3. Cut the cooled chicken into bite-size chunks. Toss with the red pepper and the Dilled Mayonnaise. (The salad can be refrigerated for several hours at this point.)

4. Before serving, bring to room temperature. Arrange the greens on individual plates or a large platter. Top with the chicken salad. Garnish with cherry tomatoes and serve.

Creamy Potato Salad with Chicken and Green Beans

**Makes
4 servings**

EVERY SUMMER, we enjoy a month of crisp, fresh green beans and sweet, juicy tomatoes from the garden. This salad is a perfect way to showcase such bounty, whether from your own backyard or from the local farmstand.
A dressing of creamy buttermilk and dill adds moist flavor without fat.

2 cups defatted chicken broth
¾ pound boneless, skinless chicken breast
6 medium-size red potatoes (1½ pounds), sliced into wedges (do not peel)
½ pound green beans, cut into 1½-inch pieces
1 red bell pepper, diced
¼ cup diced red onion
2 tablespoons minced fresh dill or 1 tablespoon dried
2 tablespoons extra-virgin olive oil or herb-flavored oil
2 tablespoons white wine vinegar
1 cup nonfat buttermilk
Salt and pepper
About 8 cups chopped lettuce or torn mixed greens
2 large tomatoes, diced

1. In a medium saucepan, bring the broth and chicken just to a boil, reduce the heat to low and poach the chicken until white and firm throughout, about 15 minutes. Remove the chicken from the broth, leaving the broth in the pan. Cool the chicken, dice and set aside.

2. Add the potatoes to the broth, adding water to cover. Cover the pan, bring to a boil, and boil gently until the potatoes are tender, about 8 minutes. Plunge into cold water to stop the cooking and drain well.

3. Blanch the green beans in boiling water to cover for 1 minute. Plunge into cold water to stop the cooking and drain well.

4. In a large salad bowl, combine the chicken, potatoes, green beans, red pepper, onion and dill. Add the oil and vinegar and toss well. Add the buttermilk and toss. Taste and adjust the seasonings, adding salt, plenty of pepper and more dill, if needed. Chill before serving.

5. Place a bed of lettuce or greens on individual plates or in a large serving bowl. Add the tomatoes to the potato salad and toss. Spoon the salad over the greens and serve.

Curried Rice and Chicken Salad with Chutney Vinaigrette

Makes
4 servings

BOLD AND EXOTIC is the only way to describe this combination of curried rice, chicken, apples, peas and mint dressed with a tangy mango vinaigrette.

2	cups uncooked white rice (preferably long-grain)
1	tablespoon peanut or canola oil
¼	cup minced onion
2	garlic cloves, minced
1	tablespoon curry powder
1	teaspoon salt
3¾	cups water
2	cups diced cooked chicken or turkey
½	green bell pepper, diced
1	cup fresh or frozen green peas
1	apple, cored and diced (do not peel)
¼	cup chopped scallions
¼	cup chopped fresh mint

Chutney Vinaigrette

¾	cup mango chutney
2	tablespoons cider vinegar
1	tablespoon peanut oil
1	teaspoon Dijon-style mustard
1	teaspoon honey

Salt and pepper

1. Wash the rice in several changes of water until the water runs clear. Drain well.

2. In a medium saucepan, heat the oil over medium heat. Add the rice, onion, garlic and curry powder. Sauté until the rice appears dry, about 4 minutes. Add the salt and the 3¾ cups water, cover and bring to a boil. Reduce the heat to low and simmer until the rice is tender and all the water is absorbed, about 15 minutes. Fluff with a fork and transfer to a large salad bowl to cool.

3. Add the chicken or turkey, green pepper, peas, apple, scallions and mint to the bowl with the rice.

4. To make the vinaigrette: Combine all the ingredients in a blender. (The salad and vinaigrette can be refrigerated in separate containers for several hours at this point.)

5. Pour the vinaigrette over the salad and toss well. Taste and season with salt and pepper as needed and serve.

Chinese Chicken Noodle Salad
with Peanut Dressing

**Makes
4 servings**

EVERY FEW MONTHS, I stock up on staples in Montreal's Chinatown—the nearest city with a large Asian population. There I find black vinegar, which is the only ingredient in this spicy, rich noodle dish that can't be located in an average supermarket. My visits always include a stop for dim sum at a favorite restaurant, which makes the shopping even more entertaining.

¾ pound boneless, skinless chicken breast
2 garlic cloves
1 1-inch piece gingerroot, sliced
6 tablespoons Chinese rice wine
1 pound fresh Chinese egg noodles or
   ¾ pound dried vermicelli
2 tablespoons sesame oil
4 tablespoons smooth peanut butter
   (reduced-fat peanut butter can be used)
3 tablespoons soy sauce or more to taste
2 tablespoons Chinese black vinegar or more to taste
1-2 teaspoons chili paste with garlic or more to taste
2 tablespoons sugar or more to taste
1 English cucumber, julienned
1 carrot, julienned
1 cup julienned scallions

1. Place the chicken in a medium saucepan and cover with water. Add the garlic, ginger and 4 tablespoons of the rice wine. Bring just to a boil, reduce the heat to low and poach the chicken until firm and white throughout, about 15 minutes. Cool in the cooking liquid.

2. Meanwhile, cook the noodles according to package directions until tender but firm to the bite, 2 to 3 minutes for fresh, about 5 minutes for dried. Drain and rinse with cold water. Toss with 1 tablespoon of the sesame oil.

3. In a blender, combine the peanut butter with ½ cup of the chicken-cooking liquid. Add the remaining 2 tablespoons rice wine, the remaining 1 tablespoon sesame oil, the soy sauce, vinegar, 1 teaspoon chili paste and sugar. Blend well. Dip a noodle in the sauce to taste for seasoning, and add more chili paste as needed.

4. Remove the chicken from the cooking liquid and julienne. (The chicken, noodles and dressing can be refrigerated in separate containers for several hours at this point.)

5. Before serving, bring the noodles and dressing to room temperature. In a large salad bowl, combine the chicken, noodles and dressing. Toss well. Taste and adjust the seasonings, adding more soy sauce, vinegar, chili paste or sugar as needed. Arrange the vegetables on top and serve.

BLACK VINEGAR is available from
    Uwajimaya
    P.O. Box 3003
    Seattle, WA 98114
    (206) 624-6248.
You can substitute Worcestershire sauce, but the flavor is significantly different.

Tropical Chicken Salad

Makes
4 servings

THE ADDITION of fruit, lime juice and cilantro transforms a fairly traditional chicken salad into a tropical dish. Allspice continues the theme.

4	cups chopped cooked chicken
1	red or green bell pepper, diced
1	carrot, grated
1	cup diced celery
1	cup well-drained canned crushed pineapple
1	cup well-drained canned chopped mandarin oranges
½	cup chopped scallions
½	cup fat-free mayonnaise
½	cup fat-free sour cream
2-3	tablespoons chopped fresh cilantro
2	tablespoons fresh lime juice
2	garlic cloves, minced
1	teaspoon ground allspice
	Salt and pepper
8	cups torn mixed salad greens

1. In a large bowl, combine the chicken, bell pepper, carrot, celery, pineapple, mandarin oranges and scallions. Toss to mix.

2. In a small bowl, combine the mayonnaise, sour cream, cilantro, lime juice, garlic and allspice. (The salad and dressing can be refrigerated in separate containers for several hours at this point.)

3. Just before serving, add the dressing to the chicken salad and toss well. Season with salt and pepper to taste. Serve on a bed of greens on individual plates or in a serving bowl.

Herbed Turkey Barley Salad

1	cup pearled barley
3	cups water
1¾	cups diced smoked turkey breast (½ pound)
1	15-ounce can black beans, rinsed and drained
1	carrot, diced
½	cup diced red onion
½	cup chopped fresh parsley
1	tablespoon chopped fresh mint
1	tablespoon chopped fresh basil or cilantro
3	tablespoons extra-virgin olive oil
1	tablespoon white wine vinegar
	Salt and pepper to taste

Makes
4 servings

1. Place the barley in a strainer and set the strainer in a bowl. Run cold water through the barley, swishing with your hands, until the water runs clear. Drain well. Bring the 3 cups water to a boil in a medium saucepan, add the barley, cover, and return to a boil. Reduce the heat to low and simmer until the liquid is absorbed and the grains are just tender, about 30 minutes. Drain off any excess water. Fluff with a fork. Cool to room temperature.

2. In a large salad bowl, combine the cooked barley, turkey, beans, carrot, onion and herbs. Toss lightly to mix.

3. Add the oil, vinegar and generous amounts of salt and pepper. Toss and serve.

ONE OF THE FIRST cultivated grains, barley was planted in Asia around 7,000 B.C. and was the primary grain in Europe for centuries, until it was displaced by wheat. Today, barley is often neglected, perhaps because of its relatively long cooking time, 35 to 45 minutes. In this salad, the natural sweetness of the grain is complemented by black beans and smoked turkey, though leftover cooked turkey could be used instead.

Pan-Seared Turkey Salad
with Anchovy-Shallot Vinaigrette

Makes
4 servings

THE RICH, WARM
vinaigrette, flavored
with shallots and salty
anchovies, provides a tasty
contrast to a simple salad
of greens, tomatoes and
turkey. Chicken can be
substituted for the turkey.

Anchovy-Shallot Vinaigrette

½   cup defatted chicken broth

3   anchovy fillets, rinsed and patted dry

1   large shallot, chopped

2   tablespoons chopped fresh parsley

2   tablespoons red wine vinegar

1   tablespoon extra-virgin olive oil

    Salt and pepper

Turkey Salad

1   tablespoon extra-virgin olive oil

1   pound turkey breast cutlets

    Salt and pepper

12   cups torn mixed salad greens

2   large vine-ripened tomatoes, cut into chunks

1   tablespoon capers

½   cup Vidalia or similar sweet onion rings

1. To make the vinaigrette: Combine the broth, anchovies, shallot, parsley and vinegar in a blender. Blend until almost smooth. With the motor running, slowly drizzle in the oil and blend until fully incorporated. Season with salt and pepper to taste.

2. To make the turkey salad: Heat the oil in a large nonstick skillet. Add the turkey, sprinkle with salt and pepper and cook on both sides until done, about 5 minutes total. Remove the turkey from the skillet and pour in the vinaigrette. Bring to a boil; remove from the heat. Slice the turkey into thin strips.

3. Place the greens on individual plates. Arrange the turkey strips over the greens. Drizzle the warm vinaigrette on top. Scatter the tomatoes, capers and onion rings over the salads. Serve at once.

Turkey Salad
with Wild Rice and Apples

**Makes
4 servings**

THIS QUINTESSENTIAL
fall salad combines
wild rice, apples, grapes and
sweet peppers with turkey
in a creamy dressing lightly
flavored with honey
mustard. It's a great way
to use turkey after a
Thanksgiving feast, but if
you don't have the leftovers,
this is just as good made
with cooked chicken.
Cortland apples will hold
their color best.

About 2 cups cooked wild rice
(from ⅔ cup uncooked)
2   cups shredded cooked turkey
1   cup red or green seedless grapes (halved if large)
1   red bell pepper, diced
2   celery stalks, diced
¼   cup chopped fresh parsley
4   scallions, chopped
¾   cup nonfat buttermilk
½   cup reduced-fat mayonnaise
3   tablespoons fresh lemon juice
1   tablespoon honey mustard
1   pound (2 large) Cortland apples (do not peel)
Salt and pepper
8-10   cups torn mixed leafy greens

1. In a large mixing bowl, combine the rice, turkey, grapes, bell pepper, celery, parsley and scallions and toss to mix.

2. In a small bowl, combine the buttermilk, mayonnaise, lemon juice and mustard. Blend well. (The salad and dressing can be refrigerated in separate containers for several hours at this point. Bring to room temperature before continuing.)

3. Pour the dressing over the salad and toss gently.

4. Core and finely chop the apples. Add to the salad and toss to mix. Season to taste with salt and pepper.

5. Place a bed of greens on individual plates. Mound the salad on the greens and serve.

Marinated Vegetable Salad
with Smoked Turkey

Makes
4 servings

CAULIFLOWER, green beans, artichoke hearts, peppers and onions are marinated in a lemony vinaigrette. Smoked turkey, tomatoes and fresh greens are added. The resulting salad is crunchy, tasty and good for you. Serve it with sturdy Italian bread. You'll want to sop up all the vinaigrette—because it's made with chicken broth and just a touch of olive oil, it is as healthful as the salad.

Salad

2	cups small cauliflower florets (½ pound)
1	cup green beans, cut into 1-inch pieces
1	carrot, sliced
1	14-ounce can artichoke hearts, rinsed and drained
¼	cup diced red onion
½	green bell pepper, thinly sliced
2	celery stalks, sliced

Dressing

¾	cup defatted chicken broth
½	cup fresh lemon juice
1	tablespoon extra-virgin olive oil
4	garlic cloves, chopped
1	tablespoon chopped fresh oregano or
	1½ teaspoons dried
	Salt and pepper

¼	pound smoked turkey breast, diced
4	plum tomatoes, diced
10	cups torn romaine lettuce

1. To make the salad: Bring a medium saucepan full of water to a boil. Blanch the cauliflower, beans and carrot for 45 seconds. Plunge into cold water to stop the cooking and drain.

2. Place the vegetables in a large bowl and add the artichoke hearts, onion, bell pepper and celery.

3. To make the dressing: In a small bowl, whisk together all the ingredients, adding salt and pepper to taste. Pour over the salad. Cover and refrigerate for at least 4 hours or up to 8 hours, tossing occasionally.

4. Just before serving, add the smoked turkey, tomatoes and lettuce to the salad. Toss well. Taste and adjust the seasonings, adding salt and pepper as needed, and serve.

Turkey and Greens with Cranberry Vinaigrette

**Makes
4 servings**

LEFTOVER cranberry sauce, turkey and extra wild rice that didn't make it into the stuffing inspired this salad. It has since become a family favorite that I make throughout the year. A fruited vinegar and walnut oil enhance the flavor, but if you don't regularly stock those ingredients, substitute balsamic vinegar and extra-virgin olive oil.

Cranberry Vinaigrette

1   cup jellied cranberry sauce
2   shallots, chopped
2   tablespoons raspberry vinegar or other
       fruited vinegar or balsamic vinegar
2   tablespoons orange juice
4   tablespoons walnut oil or extra-virgin olive oil

Salad

3   cups cooked diced turkey
    About 2 cups cooked wild rice (from ⅔ cup uncooked)
2   celery stalks, sliced thin
½   cup thinly sliced red onion
10-12   cups torn mixed salad greens

1. To make the vinaigrette: Combine the cranberry sauce, shallots, vinegar and orange juice in a blender and process until smooth. With the motor running, slowly drizzle in the oil and process until it is completely incorporated.

2. To make the salad: Combine the turkey, wild rice, celery and onion in a large salad bowl. Pour in the vinaigrette and toss well. Add the greens, gently toss again and serve.

German-Style Potato Salad
with Turkey Sausage

Salt
2½   pounds small red potatoes, sliced ¼ inch thick
¾   pound Italian-style hot turkey sausage, casings removed
1   red bell pepper, diced
½   cup diced red or yellow onion
2   garlic cloves, minced
½   cup defatted chicken broth or water
½   cup white vinegar
2   tablespoons sugar
1   tablespoon all-purpose flour
½   teaspoon celery seeds
Freshly ground pepper

**Makes
4 servings**

FOR A CHANGE of pace, this warm salad with sweet-sour dressing is pleasing. Serve it over greens or on its own with a loaf of rye or pumpernickel bread.

1. Bring a medium saucepan full of lightly salted water to a boil. Add the potatoes, cover and boil gently until just tender, about 8 minutes. Drain.

2. In a large nonstick skillet, brown the sausage, breaking it up into small pieces as it cooks. Add the bell pepper, onion and garlic and sauté until just tender, about 3 minutes.

3. In a small bowl, combine the broth or water, vinegar, sugar, flour and celery seeds and stir until smooth. Add to the skillet and cook, stirring constantly, until thickened and bubbly. Stir in the potatoes. Season to taste with salt and pepper. Cook for 2 to 3 minutes more, stirring gently, until heated through. Serve warm.

Chapter Five

Hearty Salads *with* Meat

Roast Beef Salad *with* Potato Crispies

**Makes
4 servings**

THIS IS A SALAD of convenience, made with deli roast beef and a quick, creamy horseradish dressing. You can use all fresh vegetables or a combination of fresh and pickled ones. You can even omit the garnish of potato crispies—golden shreds of potatoes and onions crisped in a hot oven—but I think they are the best part.

Potato Crispies

1 pound (about 3 medium) potatoes
1 medium onion, finely diced
 Salt and pepper

Creamy Horseradish Dressing

¾ cup nonfat buttermilk
½ cup fat-free mayonnaise
2 tablespoons prepared horseradish
2 tablespoons chopped fresh chives
 Salt

Salad

½ pound wax beans or green beans or 1 pint dilly beans, drained
8-12 cups torn mixed salad greens
1 pound thinly sliced roast beef
4 medium tomatoes, cut into wedges
1 cup julienned pickled beets or freshly cooked or canned beets, well drained

1. Preheat the oven to 450°F.

2. To make the potato crispies: Finely grate the potatoes, using the fine shredding disk of a food processor. Rinse the potatoes well, then drain well. Spread out on a clean kitchen towel or paper towel and pat dry. Toss the onion with the potatoes. Spray a baking sheet with nonstick cooking spray. Spread the potatoes evenly on the baking sheet. Mist with cooking spray. Bake until golden, 20 to 30 minutes, or until crisp, flipping and separating the potatoes once or twice. Season to taste with salt and pepper and leave on the baking sheet until you are ready to assemble the salad.

3. To make the dressing: Combine all the ingredients in a blender and process until smooth. Taste and adjust the seasonings, adding salt if needed. Set aside.

4. To make the salad: If you are using fresh wax beans or green beans, cut them into 3-inch lengths. In a medium saucepan, blanch them in boiling water to cover for about 45 seconds. Plunge into cold water to stop the cooking, then drain well.

5. Divide greens among individual plates. Roll up the beef slices and arrange in the center of the greens, with the beans, tomatoes and beets around the edges. Spoon a little dressing over the vegetables. Sprinkle the potato crispies over the salad and serve, passing additional dressing at the table.

FOR SHREDDING the potatoes, you will get best results with a food processor, using the fine shredding disk. However, you can use the large-hole side of a box grater in a pinch. Add a few minutes to the cooking time.

Vietnamese Beef Salad

Makes
4 servings

Like many of the best Vietnamese dishes, this salad balances sweet, hot, salty and sour flavors. Strips of rare grilled steak top crunchy vegetables and cellophane noodles that are dressed with a felicitous combination of fish sauce, lime juice, sugar, hot peppers and lemongrass.

1	pound flank steak, sirloin steak or other tender cut
2	tablespoons soy sauce
2	garlic cloves, minced
3	1.75-ounce packages cellophane noodles

Dressing

½	cup fish sauce
½	cup fresh lime juice (3-4 limes)
6	tablespoons sugar
1	hot green pepper, minced
1	stem lemongrass, finely chopped
6	cups thinly sliced romaine lettuce
1	carrot, peeled, shaved into curls
1	English cucumber, julienned
¼	cup chopped fresh mint
¼	cup chopped fresh cilantro

1. Rub the steak with soy sauce and garlic; set aside.

2. Prepare a medium-hot fire in a charcoal or gas grill, with the rack set 3 to 4 inches above the coals, or preheat the broiler.

3. Soak the cellophane noodles in hot water to soften, about 5 minutes. Drain and set aside.

4. To make the dressing: Combine all the ingredients in a small saucepan. Heat, stirring, until the sugar dissolves. Set aside to cool.

5. On individual plates, make a bed of lettuce. On top of the lettuce, arrange the cellophane noodles, then the carrot curls, cucumber, mint and cilantro, reserving a few tablespoons of the herbs for a garnish.

6. When the coals are medium-hot, grill the steak, turning once, until it reaches the desired doneness. A ½-inch-thick steak will take about 3 minutes per side for medium-rare. Let rest a minute, then slice into thin strips.

7. Pour the dressing over the salad. Lay the strips of warm steak on top. Serve at once.

LEMONGRASS, which gives Southeast Asian dishes a characteristic sour-lemon flavor and fragrance, is gray-green in color, somewhat woody in texture and resembles a scallion. Stock up on it and keep the extra in an airtight bag in the freezer. Use only the bottom 4 inches. In a pinch, ¼ teaspoon of finely grated lemon zest can be substituted for a stem of lemongrass, but the taste is not the same.

Taco Salad

**Makes
4 servings**

I FELL IN LOVE with taco salads the first time I tasted that irresistible combination of crispy salad drenched in chili, sour cream and guacamole, placed in a bowl formed by a deep-fried tortilla. It was a sad day when the Center for Science in the Public Interest published their findings that this dish typically packs in more fat than a couple of burgers from a fast-food joint. Well, who wants to bother with the fuss of deep-frying a tortilla anyhow?

1	small onion, finely chopped
¾	pound lean ground beef
2	tablespoons chili powder
1½	teaspoons ground cumin
1	15-ounce can kidney beans, rinsed and drained
1	15-ounce can diced tomatoes
	Salt and pepper
12	cups chopped iceberg lettuce
½	English cucumber, sliced
¼	cup chopped red onion
4	plum tomatoes, chopped
2	tablespoons fresh lemon juice
1	teaspoon extra-virgin olive oil
½	cup reduced-fat Cheddar or Monterey Jack cheese
3	ounces baked tortilla chips (about 40)
¼	cup fat-free sour cream
¼	cup chopped fresh or canned green chilies

1. Heat a large nonstick skillet over medium-high heat. Add the onion, ground beef, chili powder and cumin and cook until the meat no longer shows any pink, stirring frequently. Drain the mixture in a colander to remove excess fat. Return the mixture to the skillet and add the beans, tomatoes and salt and pepper to taste. Keep warm.

2. In a large bowl, combine the lettuce, cucumber, red onion and tomatoes. Add lemon juice, oil and salt and pepper to taste. Toss well.

3. Serve the salad on individual plates. Top with the cheese, then the warm chili mixture. Garnish each plate with the tortilla chips. Top each serving with a dollop of sour cream and some chopped chilies.

THIS VERSION replaces the usual fried tortilla with baked tortilla chips. The result is a delicious, easy-to-make salad that is significantly reduced in fat.

Pita *and* Beef Salad

**Makes
4 servings**

THE TUSCANS have their panzanella, the Arabs their fettoush— salads that make clever use of leftover bread. In the classic fettoush, torn strips of pita pockets, romaine lettuce, cucumbers, tomatoes and herbs are tossed in a lemony vinaigrette. In this version, chickpeas, grilled steak and onions transform the simple fettoush into a hearty dinner.

1   pound London broil or other tender cut of steak
1   large onion, quartered
4   toasted pita pockets
16 cups torn romaine lettuce
3   medium tomatoes, chopped
½   English cucumber, quartered and sliced
1   15-ounce can chickpeas, rinsed and drained

Lemon-Mint Dressing
¼   cup fresh mint leaves
¼   cup chopped fresh parsley
2   garlic cloves, chopped
3   tablespoons fresh lemon juice
3   tablespoons defatted chicken broth
2   tablespoons extra-virgin olive oil or herb-flavored oil

1. Prepare a medium-hot fire in a charcoal or gas grill, with the rack 3 to 4 inches above the coals, or preheat the broiler. Cook the meat and the onion for 4 to 5 minutes, then turn and cook 3 to 4 minutes more for medium. Set aside. Toast the pita pockets and slice into thin strips.

2. In a large bowl, mix the pita with the remaining salad ingredients.

3. To make the dressing: Process all the ingredients in a blender.

4. Slice the meat into thin strips, chop the onion and add both to the salad. Pour the dressing over the salad, toss and serve.

Tomato Salad
with Prosciutto and Basil

3	pounds vine-ripened tomatoes, chopped
1	19-ounce can cannellini beans, rinsed and drained
1	Vidalia or similar sweet onion, thinly sliced
4	ounces prosciutto, chopped
½	cup chopped fresh basil
4	garlic cloves, minced
2	tablespoons extra-virgin olive oil or herb-flavored oil
2	tablespoons fresh lemon juice
	Salt and pepper
1	head Boston lettuce
2	cups watercress or arugula, tough stems removed
3	cups Garlic Croutons (page 155)

**Makes
4 servings**

1. A few hours or at least 30 minutes before serving, combine the tomatoes, beans, onion, prosciutto, basil, garlic, oil and lemon juice in a large bowl. Season with salt and pepper to taste. Set aside to marinate.

2. Just before serving, arrange the lettuce on a platter or individual plates. Add the watercress or arugula and croutons to the tomato mixture and toss to mix. Spoon the salad onto the lettuce and serve.

ONLY VINE-RIPENED tomatoes will do for this lush salad. The sweet tomatoes combined with the salty, rich prosciutto and the sharp green tones of the basil, watercress and garlic make for a meal of uncommon luxury—especially for one that derives fewer than 25 percent of its calories from fat. With a glass of red wine, you have a feast.

Gazpacho Salad *with* Cumin-Crusted Grilled Pork

**Makes
4 servings**

With vine-ripened tomatoes, very little dressing is needed to create a flavor explosion. The traditional vegetables in gazpacho—tomatoes, peppers, onion and cucumber—make a bed for cumin-scented grilled pork slices. The toasted bread is absolutely necessary for sopping up all the lovely tomato juices.

Pork

1	teaspoon ground cumin
½	teaspoon sugar
½	teaspoon salt
¼	teaspoon chili powder
¼	teaspoon ground allspice
1	pound pork tenderloin

Gazpacho Salad

3	large vine-ripened tomatoes, cubed
1	red bell pepper, diced
1	green bell pepper, diced
1	yellow bell pepper, diced
1	cucumber, preferably unpeeled, seeded and diced
½	red onion, diced
1	celery stalk, diced
¼	cup chopped fresh parsley
2	tablespoons red wine vinegar
1	tablespoon extra-virgin olive oil
	Salt and pepper to taste
8	long, narrow slices French bread, cut on the diagonal
	Romaine lettuce

1. To make the pork: At least 1 hour before serving, combine the cumin, sugar, salt, chili powder and allspice in a small bowl. Rub into the pork and set aside in the refrigerator.

2. To make the gazpacho salad: Combine the tomatoes, bell peppers, cucumber, onion, celery and parsley in a large bowl. Add the vinegar, oil and salt and pepper and toss well. Taste and add more salt, if needed. Set aside for at least 1 hour.

3. Prepare a medium-hot fire in a charcoal or gas grill with the rack set 3 to 4 inches above the coals.

4. When the coals are medium-hot, grill the pork for 7 to 9 minutes per side, or until an instant-read thermometer registers 150° to 165°F. Let the meat rest for a few minutes. Meanwhile, lightly grill the bread until golden, turning once. Slice the meat thinly.

5. Line individual plates with the lettuce. Spoon the gazpacho salad on top. Arrange the pork slices over the salad. Place the toasted bread on the side of each plate. Serve at once.

Cowboy Pork *and* Bean Salad

Makes

4 servings

I'M WILLING TO GUESS no cowboy was lucky enough to be served this grub—pork tenderloin on a bed of greens, beans, chips and corn. But most of the ingredients might have been found in a chuck wagon, and the salad does make a tasty campfire meal.

Bean Salad

1   15-ounce can black beans, rinsed and drained
1   15-ounce can pinto beans, rinsed and drained
1   cup fresh or frozen corn kernels (thawed if frozen)
1   cup diced fresh tomato
1   green bell pepper, diced
¼   cup diced red onion
1   small hot red or green pepper, diced (optional)
¼   cup chopped fresh parsley
2   tablespoons chopped fresh cilantro
1   recipe Spicy Tomato Vinaigrette (page 148)

Pork

½   pound pork tenderloin
1   teaspoon ground chili powder
1   teaspoon ground cumin
2   tablespoons fresh lime juice

About 6 cups torn lettuce or torn mixed greens
3   ounces baked tortilla chips (about 40)

1. Prepare a medium-hot fire in a charcoal or gas grill, with the rack set 3 to 4 inches above the coals, or preheat the broiler.

2. To make the bean salad: In a large bowl, combine the beans, corn, tomato, bell pepper, onion, hot pepper (if using), parsley and cilantro. Pour the vinaigrette over the vegetables, toss and set aside.

3. To make the pork: Slice the pork into ½-inch-thick slices. Combine the chili powder, cumin and lime juice and brush on the meat. When the grill or broiler is ready, grill or broil the meat, turning once, until medium, 2 to 3 minutes per side. Do not overcook. Cut into strips.

4. To serve, place a bed of lettuce on individual serving plates. Mound the bean salad in the center. Lay the pork strips over the beans. Garnish with the tortilla chips.

Warm Lamb Salad
with Tomatoes and Feta

**Makes
4 servings**

In Vermont, where I live, sheep once outnumbered the people six to one. Those days are long gone, but the industry is making a comeback with tender spring lambs. The ideal cut for grilling is the tenderloin, but that can be expensive and hard to find. An alternative is to have your butcher butterfly a leg of lamb and divide it into 1-pound portions.

Lamb

1	pound lamb tenderloins or butterflied leg of lamb
1	teaspoon ground cumin
1	teaspoon garlic powder
1	teaspoon paprika
½	teaspoon ground cinnamon
½	teaspoon salt

Salad

3	medium-to-large tomatoes, diced
1½	cups cooked chickpeas, rinsed and drained
½	red onion, thinly sliced
¼	cup chopped fresh mint
2	tablespoons extra-virgin olive oil
3	tablespoons fresh lemon juice
⅓	cup crumbled feta cheese
	Salt and pepper
6	cups torn mixed salad greens

1. To make the lamb: Trim the fat from the lamb. Combine the cumin, garlic powder, paprika, cinnamon and salt in a small bowl. Rub on the lamb and let marinate for at least 30 minutes at room temperature or up to 8 hours in the refrigerator.

2. Prepare a medium-hot fire in a charcoal or gas grill, with the rack set 3 to 4 inches above the coals.

3. To make the salad: Combine the tomatoes, chickpeas, onion and mint in a large salad bowl. Toss to mix. Drizzle in the oil, lemon juice and feta cheese. Toss to mix, season to taste with salt and pepper and set aside.

4. When the coals are medium-hot, grill the lamb, turning once, until rare and the internal temperature reaches 140°F on an instant-read thermometer, about 5 minutes per side. Let the lamb rest for 10 minutes before thinly slicing.

5. Arrange a bed of greens on individual plates. Spoon the tomato salad on top. Arrange the lamb slices on top of the salad. Serve at once.

Couscous Salad *with* Lamb

**Makes
4 servings**

FOR THIS SALAD, lamb is marinated in charmoula, a Moroccan pesto made with parsley, cilantro, cinnamon, cumin and ginger. It is then grilled and served on a bed of couscous. Couscous itself tastes mild, but when combined with sharp lemon, mint, salty olives and parsley, it takes on a bold flavor.

Lamb

1	pound lamb tenderloins or butterflied leg of lamb
¼	cup chopped fresh parsley
¼	cup chopped fresh cilantro
1	teaspoon ground cumin
½	teaspoon ground cinnamon
½	teaspoon ground ginger
½	teaspoon dried thyme
1	tablespoon extra-virgin olive oil

Couscous

1½	cups instant couscous
2¼	cups boiling water
1	cup chopped fresh parsley
¼	cup chopped fresh mint
2	large tomatoes, diced
1	English cucumber, diced
4	scallions, chopped
½	cup brined Greek olives, pitted, if desired
3	tablespoons extra-virgin olive oil
	Juice of 1 lemon, or more to taste
	Salt and pepper

1. To make the lamb: Trim the fat from the lamb. In a food processor, combine the parsley, cilantro and spices. With the motor running, drizzle in the oil to make a paste. Rub the paste onto the lamb. Set aside to marinate for at least 30 minutes at room temperature or up to 8 hours in the refrigerator.

2. Prepare a medium-hot fire in a charcoal or gas grill with the rack set 3 to 4 inches above the coals.

3. To make the couscous: Combine the couscous and boiling water in a large bowl. Cover and let stand until the couscous is tender and the water is absorbed, about 10 minutes. Fluff with a fork and cool to room temperature.

4. Add the parsley, mint, tomatoes, cucumber, scallions and olives to the couscous. Toss to mix. Drizzle in the oil, lemon juice and season with salt and pepper to taste. Toss to mix and set aside.

5. When the coals are medium-hot, grill the lamb, turning once, until rare and the internal temperature reaches 140°F on an instant-read thermometer, about 5 minutes per side. Let the lamb rest for 10 minutes before thinly slicing.

6. Arrange a bed of the couscous salad on individual plates or one large platter. Place the lamb slices on top. Serve at once.

Chapter Six

Dressings *and* Croutons

Roasted Garlic Vinaigrette

**Makes
about ¾ cup**

Roasting mellows the garlic and brings out a sweet, nutty flavor. This dressing is richly flavored but not overpowering. It goes well with Caesar salads.

1   whole garlic bulb
About ¼ cup defatted chicken broth or water
3   tablespoons extra-virgin olive oil
3   tablespoons white wine
1   tablespoon red wine vinegar
Salt to taste

1. Preheat the oven to 450°F.

2. Remove the papery outer skin from the garlic bulbs. Slice off the top of the bulb to expose the tips of the cloves. Place the bulb in a small ovenproof bowl and pour the broth or water over. Roast for about 30 minutes, basting once or twice, or until the cloves are soft and browned. Remove the garlic from the liquid and let cool. (If you are in a hurry, separate the cloves to speed the cooling process.)

3. When the garlic is cool enough to handle, squeeze out the cloves from the skins. In the blender, combine the garlic with the remaining ingredients. Process until smooth. (Stored in an airtight container, the vinaigrette will keep for 3 to 4 days in the refrigerator.)

Chipotle Vinaigrette

1 teaspoon chipotles en adobo, or more to taste
(for a mail-order source, see page 45)
1 garlic clove, minced
1 tablespoon chopped fresh cilantro
1 tablespoon chopped fresh parsley
¼ cup white wine vinegar or champagne vinegar
¼ cup defatted chicken broth
1 teaspoon maple syrup
1 tablespoon olive oil
Salt

Combine 1 teaspoon chipotles en adobo, the garlic, cilantro, parsley, vinegar, broth and maple syrup in a blender. With the motor running, slowly drizzle in the oil. Add salt to taste and additional chipotles en adobo, if needed. (Stored in an airtight container, the vinaigrette will keep for 4 to 5 days in the refrigerator.) Stir or shake well just before using.

Makes about ½ cup

THIS SPICY vinaigrette gets a punch of flavor from the chipotles en adobo, a blend of smoke-dried jalapeños, onions, garlic and spices in an oil-and-vinegar base. The hearty dressing goes particularly well with meat and poultry. Try it on a composed salad with grilled steak, pork tenderloin or chicken. Or use it to dress a black-bean or corn-and-pepper salad. An opened jar of chipotles en adobo will lose potency over time, so be sure to taste the vinaigrette before using.

Citrus Vinaigrette

**Makes
about ⅔ cup**

Orange, lemon and basil form the foundation of this light vinaigrette. Seafood salads have a special affinity for it, but it is also good on a green salad.

⅓ cup fresh orange juice
2 tablespoons chopped fresh basil
1 tablespoon fresh lemon juice
1 teaspoon grated orange zest
½ teaspoon grated lemon zest
2 tablespoons extra-virgin olive oil

In a small bowl, combine the orange juice, basil, lemon juice and zests. Whisk in the oil. (This vinaigrette is best used immediately, but stored in an airtight container, it will keep for 2 days in the refrigerator.)

Creamy Nonfat Celery Seed Dressing

Makes ¾ cup

My kids think this creamy dressing doesn't taste homemade (a compliment in their world). Slightly sweet, it is a good match for carrot, cabbage or spinach salads.

¼ cup pure maple syrup
¼ cup cider vinegar
¼ cup plain nonfat yogurt
¼ teaspoon celery seed
Salt to taste

Combine all the ingredients in a jar and shake well. (Stored in an airtight container, the dressing will keep for about 1 week in the refrigerator.) Shake well before using.

Mango Chutney Vinaigrette

¾ cup mango chutney
2 tablespoons fresh lemon juice
1 tablespoon peanut oil
1 teaspoon honey
¼ cup chopped fresh mint
¼ cup chopped fresh cilantro
Salt to taste

Combine all the ingredients in a blender and puree until smooth. Taste and adjust the seasonings. (Stored in an airtight container, the vinaigrette will keep for 4 to 5 days in the refrigerator.) Stir or shake well just before using.

Makes about 1¼ cups

CHUTNEY IS A SPICY condiment that contains fruit, vinegar, sugar and spices. Major Grey mango chutney is one of the most popular commercial brands. Having some on hand may inspire you to spread it on cheese sandwiches or turkey burgers or make this memorable sweet-sour vinaigrette. It provides a tangy contrast to curried rice. Add a few vegetables, and you have a vivacious salad. The dressing is also delightful on greens.

Spicy Tomato Vinaigrette

**Makes
about ½ cup**

COMBINE THIS SPICY dressing, which has a Southwestern flair, with a can of black beans for an instant salad.

2   tablespoons canola oil
2   tablespoons fresh lime juice
2   tablespoons ketchup
1   tablespoon white wine vinegar
2   teaspoons sugar
1   teaspoon chili powder
½   teaspoon ground cumin
2   garlic cloves, minced
    Salt and pepper to taste

Whisk together the ingredients. (Stored in an airtight container, the vinaigrette will keep in the refrigerator for several weeks.) Stir or shake well just before using.

Caesar Salad Dressing

6   ounces silken or soft tofu

¼   cup water

1   2-ounce can flat anchovy fillets packed in oil, undrained

2   garlic cloves, chopped

3   tablespoons red wine vinegar

1   teaspoon Dijon-style mustard

Combine all the ingredients in a blender and process until smooth. (This dressing is best used immediately, but leftovers may be refrigerated in an airtight container for 3 to 4 days.)

Makes about 1½ cups

FOR YEARS, I avoided Caesar salads because of the high percentage of calories from fat and the raw egg. In this dressing, both problems are solved by tofu, which gives a surprisingly creamy result. All I can say is, try it!

Buttermilk-Dill Dressing

Makes about ¾ cup

THE FLAVOR OF DILL dominates this silkily thin dressing. Serve it on mixed greens. It works well in potato salads, too.

½ cup nonfat buttermilk
1 garlic clove
1 scallion, chopped
1 tablespoon minced fresh dill
1½ teaspoons extra-virgin olive oil
1½ teaspoons white wine vinegar
Salt and freshly ground pepper to taste

Combine all the ingredients in a blender and process until smooth. (The dressing is best used immediately, but leftovers may be refrigerated in an airtight container for 3 to 4 days.)

Japanese Tamari-Sesame Dressing

Makes ½ cup

THIS LIGHT DRESSING is fantastic with raw or lightly blanched vegetables. It keeps well.

3 tablespoons tamari
3 tablespoons rice wine vinegar
1 tablespoon mirin (sweet Japanese wine)
1 tablespoon sugar
1 tablespoon sesame oil

Combine all the ingredients and mix well. (Stored in an airtight container in the refrigerator, the dressing will keep for several weeks.) Stir or shake well just before using.

Lemon-Soy Dressing

½ cup soy sauce
¼ cup water
¼ cup sesame oil
6 tablespoons fresh lemon juice
4 garlic cloves, minced

Combine all the ingredients and shake well. This dressing separates quickly, so be sure to shake it immediately before using.

Makes about 1 cup

THIS pleasing blend is quick to make, low in fat, keeps forever and is very, very good. I especially like it on spinach salads.

Catalina Dressing

½ cup ketchup
⅓ cup water
3 tablespoons red wine vinegar
2 tablespoons olive oil
2 tablespoons finely chopped onion
2 tablespoons sugar
2 garlic cloves, minced
  Salt and pepper to taste

Combine all the ingredients in a blender and process until smooth. Taste and adjust the seasonings. (Stored in an airtight container, the dressing will keep for about 2 weeks in the refrigerator.) Stir or shake well just before using.

Makes 1¼ cups

AH, THE SWEET-SOUR dressing of my youth, wonderful on a crunchy wedge of iceberg lettuce. I still love it! In this version, the fat is significantly reduced, but the flavor remains as I remember it.

Sesame Garlic Dressing

**Makes
about ¾ cup**

I'VE SAMPLED enough virtuous health foods to be wary of anything tofu-based. But I was astounded by how rich and creamy this one tastes. It is great on greens and makes a wonderful dressing for cold noodles.

½   pound silken or soft tofu
1   tablespoon rice wine vinegar
1   teaspoon sesame oil
4   teaspoons soy sauce
4   garlic cloves

Combine all the ingredients in a blender or food processor. Process until smooth. (Stored in an airtight container, the dressing will keep for up to 5 days in the refrigerator.) Thin with a little water if it is too thick to pour.

Master Recipe *for* Herbal Vinegar

1   cup fresh herbs or ¼ cup chopped garlic
2   cups white wine vinegar

**Makes
2 cups**

1. Sterilize a jar in a dishwasher or by boiling in water to cover for 10 minutes. Lightly bruise or crush the herbs to release the flavors. Add to the sterilized jar.

2. Heat the vinegar until hot, not boiling, in a nonreactive saucepan. Pour the vinegar over the herbs. Cover the bottle with a nonmetallic lid. You can use plastic wrap secured with a rubber band.

3. Let the vinegar steep for about 2 weeks, shaking the bottle occasionally.

4. After 2 weeks, strain the vinegar through a coffee filter or cheesecloth and pour into a freshly sterilized bottle. Add a fresh sprig of herbs to identify the type of flavoring. Cork or cap the bottle and store in a cool, dark place for up to 6 months.

RATHER THAN PAY a premium for herbal vinegars at your specialty food store, you can easily make your own.

Recommended herbs are basil, chives, garlic, thyme, tarragon and sage.

Easy Croutons

Makes 4 cups

THE MAIN FUNCTION of a crouton is to absorb the flavor of the dressing in a salad. These easy, very low-fat croutons do that job well.

1   pound loaf of slightly stale French or Italian bread,
        cut into ¾-inch cubes (about 8 cups)
    Garlic powder, garlic salt or seasoned salt (optional)

1. Preheat the broiler.

2. Lightly spray a baking sheet with olive-oil nonstick cooking spray. Arrange the bread cubes on the baking sheet and spray lightly with the cooking spray. Sprinkle with garlic powder, garlic salt or seasoned salt, if desired. Broil until golden brown, turning once, 2 to 3 minutes per side. Let cool. (Stored in an airtight container, the croutons will keep for 2 weeks in the refrigerator or in the freezer for up to 2 months.)

Garlic Croutons

4 whole garlic bulbs
½ cup defatted chicken broth
1 tablespoon extra-virgin olive oil
¼ teaspoon salt
1 pound loaf of slightly stale French or Italian bread,
    cut into ¾-inch cubes (about 8 cups)

**Makes
about 8 cups**

1. Preheat the oven to 450°F.

2. Remove the papery outer skin from the garlic bulbs. Slice off the top to expose the tips of the cloves. Place the bulbs in a single layer in a small ovenproof bowl. Pour over ¼ cup of the broth. Roast for about 30 minutes, basting once or twice, until the cloves are very soft and browned. Remove from the broth to cool.

3. When the garlic is cool enough to handle, squeeze out the cloves from the skins. In a small bowl or a food processor, combine the garlic with the broth left in the bowl, the remaining ¼ cup broth, the oil and salt. Mash well with a fork or process to a smooth paste.

4. With your hands, toss the bread cubes with the garlic puree to coat.

5. Spray a baking sheet with nonstick cooking spray. Arrange the bread cubes in a single layer on the baking sheet. Spray the cubes with cooking spray. Bake for about 15 minutes, stirring occasionally, until lightly browned. Let cool. (Stored in an airtight container, the croutons will keep for 1 week in the refrigerator or in the freezer for up to 2 months.)

WHENEVER I MAKE these crunchy, garlicky croutons, I leave them out to cool for a few hours before storing them in a glass jar. Upon my return to the kitchen, I often find at least half of them gone. They are irresistible.

Index